reflections & voices

Reflections in the water I see
Six pretty girls on my mind today
Yellow foam floating down the river
Voices I hear of Yolŋu heroes

Verse 1, 'Mainstream'
Mandawuy Yunupiŋu, 1986

in memoriam

Milkayŋu Dolmana Munuŋgurr

Narripapa Yunupiŋu

Yomunu Yunupiŋu

reflections & voices

exploring the music of Yothu Yindi
with Mandawuy Yunupiŋu

Aaron Corn

with contributions by Marcia Langton,
Allan Marett, Melinda Sawers
& Galarrwuy Yunupiŋu

SYDNEY UNIVERSITY PRESS

First published 2009 by SYDNEY UNIVERSITY PRESS
www.sup.usyd.edu.au

Published in cooperation with Yothu Yindi and the Yothu Yindi Foundation.

All original images reproduced with permission from their identified copyright holders at the time of publication.
'A legacy of hope' recorded by Sally Treloyn in 2005, transcribed and edited by Aaron Corn, and published with permission.
Interviews with Mandawuy Yunupiŋu in 'voices' recorded in 2001, transcribed and edited by Aaron Corn.
Song lyrics translated by Aaron Corn and Mandawuy Yunupiŋu.
Musical transcriptions by Aaron Corn and Melinda Sawers.
Publishing rights for all songs transcribed are controlled by Mushroom Music Publishing and reproduced with permission.
Publishing rights for 'Treaty' are controlled by Universal Music Publishing and reproduced with permission.

Readers are advised that laws can exist in Indigenous Australian communities against speaking names and displaying images of the deceased. Please check with Indigenous elders before using this publication in their local communities.

National Library of Australia Cataloguing-in-Publication entry

Author:	Corn, Aaron David Samuel.
Title:	Reflections & voices : exploring the music of Yothu Yindi with Mandawuy Yunupingu / Aaron Corn.
ISBN:	9781920899349 (pbk.)
Notes:	Bibliography.
Subjects:	Yunupingu, Mandawuy.
	Yothu Yindi (Musical group)
	Rock music--Australia.
	Aboriginal Australians--Music.

Dewey Number: 781.660994

Cover photograph by Scott H. Welsh
Cover design by Evan Shapiro, the University Publishing Service

contents

foreword

Allan Marett

I am delighted that *Reflections & voices: exploring the music of Yothu Yindi with Mandawuy Yunupiŋu* is the first book in the National Recording Project for Indigenous Performance in Australia's series, The Indigenous Music of Australia. It is most appropriate that a volume focusing on the musical contributions and vision of Mandawuy Yunupiŋu should commence this series, since it was Mandawuy who gave the original impetus to the National Recording Project and its associated books and CDs.

The National Recording Project emanated directly from a remarkable symposium that Mandawuy led in 2002 at the Yothu Yindi Foundation's Yirrŋa Music Development Centre at Gunyaŋara. Also supported by the Australian Institute for Aboriginal and Torres Strait Islander Studies (AIATSIS), this Symposium on Indigenous Music and Dance was conceived of as a conversation between Indigenous and non-Indigenous musicians and researchers. But it was Mandawuy who gave this conversation the particular focus that led to the creation of the National Recording Project as a new initiative aimed as preserving Australia's highly endangered Indigenous song and dance traditions.

Mandawuy created this focus by choosing as our principal objective the of study an endangered *Manikay* series centred around the ancestral *marrpan* 'flatback turtle'. It was an inspired choice, which directed our attention not only to the beauty and complexity of Aboriginal song, but also to the highly endangered nature of all Indigenous musical traditions in Australia. Prior to the symposium, Mandawuy had gathered together archival recordings of *marrpan* songs for us to hear. He also arranged live *Manikay* performances by Gurrutjiri and Djalu Gurruwiwi, which we recorded and studied alongside these archival recordings. It was Mandawuy who transcribed, translated and explained each individual song, imparting just the right level of knowledge appropriate to our particular gathering.

Our views about what represents appropriate and necessary documentation of songs and dances through the National Recording Project were established at this first symposium, and refined in meetings over subsequent years. We agreed that the owners and performers of songs and dances should determine what is recorded, how it is documented, who has access to it, how it is archived and what, if any, commercial uses are made of it. Moving forward to 2009, the National Recording Project is striving to empower local communities further by training local Indigenous people to record, document and archive their own traditions.

Towards the first symposium's end in 2002, we were treated to an unforgettable unplugged version of a new Yothu Yindi song about *marrpan* that Mandawuy had just recently composed. It demonstrated how the traditional arts can survive, not only through the reproduction of traditional practices, but also through their transformation into new media. This indeed was the fundamental rationale behind the creation of Yothu Yindi: to reproduce traditional knowledge in forms that would draw local youth into the sphere of traditional knowledge. The extent to which Yothu Yindi's songs have drawn a much wider national and international audience into contact with Indigenous culture and given voice to a broad range of Indigenous political concerns is a testimony to the extraordinary reach and breadth of Mandawuy's vision.

Many voices were heard at the 2002 symposium, both Indigenous and non-Indigenous. And not only did we talk. We sang, danced and listened. And we also learned from one another. This was the first of what has become an annual Symposium on Indigenous Music and Dance that the National Recording Project organises to stimulate productive dialogues about the Indigenous performing arts among Indigenous and non-Indigenous performers and intellectuals.

But this first symposium led by Mandawuy remains very special. When at the end we asked local Indigenous elders and community members what they would most like to come out of future collaborations between researchers and performers, their answer was clear and is articulated in the Garma Statement on Indigenous Music and Performance. It called for:

1. the creation of local Indigenous knowledge centres where recordings of songs and dances could be made available in digital form

2. the establishment a National Recording Project that with appropriate Indigenous direction could systematically record, document and archive Indigenous songs and dances

3. the integration such a project's outcomes into broader community initiatives in the areas of health, education and governance

4. the publication of recordings of Indigenous songs 'in order to educate the broader Australian public and international audiences about Aboriginal performance traditions' (Yunupiŋu, Langton & Marett, 2002).

The Indigenous Music of Australia book and CD series is a response to this last proposal. *Reflections & voices: exploring the music of Yothu Yindi with Mandawuy Yunupiŋu* not only ensures a better understanding of Indigenous music, but also represents a genuine collaboration between author Aaron Corn and the visionary Mandawuy Yunupiŋu.

Future books and CDs currently planned for this series will focus on traditional genres such the *Wangga, Djanba* and *Lirrga* traditions of the Daly region, the *Kunborrk* traditions of western Arnhem Land, and the *Manikay* of central and eastern Arnhem Land. All will be inspired by this same spirit of collaboration between Indigenous and non-Indigenous partners, and by a desire to make available to as wide an audience as possible all the glorious yet fragile song and dance traditions that Indigenous owners and performers wish to share.

Mandawuy Yunupiŋu

I'd like to thank the many people who've supported Yothu Yindi over the years. Thanks to my family for their support and encouragement, and in particular to my wife, Yalmay Marika, who guided me in my work as a principal and as a songwriter. Yothu Yindi is a tribute. It reflects my understanding and deep respect for our elders, who saw the right direction and embraced the future.

It's wonderful to have performed in Yothu Yindi with so many talented musicians. My early gigs in Darwin with my great friends, Stu Kellaway, Cal Williams, Andy Beletty, and my nephews, Witiyana Marika and Milkayŋu Munuŋgurr, still stand out for me as some of the most memorable. Twenty-three years on, it's great to see how international tastes for Yolŋu music have grown, and continue to grow with the popularity of Gurrumul Yunupiŋu, who began his career in Yothu Yindi. Also deserving of special mention for his drive and commitment is my good friend Alan James who managed the band from the beginning.

I've chosen to dedicate this book to Yothu Yindi's outstanding *yiḏaki* masters, the late Milkayŋu Munuŋgurr, Narripapa Yunupiŋu and Yomunu Yunupiŋu. Though their sudden losses are still recent, I wanted their images kept here in this book, so we can see them and be reminded of the great talents they were known for in life. And also so we can be reminded of their complexities and of our failure to care for their special needs.

On a brighter note, I hope that everyone enjoys this book and thank Aaron Corn for giving it life. I hope that it will help everyone understand the richness of Yolŋu musical expression, and the centrality of language and ceremony to the continuation of our culture. Yothu Yindi would have been impossible without my own training in traditional language, song and dance. It is imperative that these traditions continue and that this fundamental cause be above politics.

Galarrwuy Yunupiŋu

Yothu Yindi was a one and only. It will never be repeated. It presented the first Australian music, a true Australian music, and all the ancestral intelligence behind it in a contemporary way for a global audience. There was never anything like it before. There is nothing like it now. And there never again will be. The land of Australia in its fullness was revealed through Yothu Yindi's music. It spoke of the past, present and future of this country and its people. It was the first truly Australian band to grace the international stage, and it gave everyone a glimpse of what Australia is all about.

Anybody who was wide awake at a Yothu Yindi show will have listened to Mandawuy's words, heard the band's songs, and in particular, felt the sound of the *yidaki*. This instrument among all others speaks loudest, even without amplification. It strictly declares Yolŋu ownership of everything that is ours through our ancestry, past, present and future. This ancestral music identifies who we are. I have observed at Yothu Yindi concerts that you can hear this tribal voice, loud and clear, in the droning of the *yidaki* from the stage, and in the crowd rising to meet it. Never in anyone else's concerts have I experienced this. Never have I seen another instrument that will make you stand up on your toes. It is the sound of Arnhem Land.

The simple breath and clever tongue work. This beautiful sound of Arnhem Land's own instrument was articulated in Yothu Yindi by my very own *waku* 'sister's child', the only boy among six girls. So I draw this preface to a close by saying that Mandawuy rightfully dedicates this book to the late Dolmana, and to the two late Maralitja men that he trained to follow him in the band. They gave voice to this instrument. And their voices echo throughout eternity.

acknowledgements

It has been a great privilege to work with Mandawuy Yunupiŋu on this book since 2001. On my various visits to their homelands in Arnhem Land, Mandawuy and his family have always been welcoming and for this I am truly grateful. Mandawuy's wife, Yalmay Marika, and daughter, Guḻumbu Yunupiŋu, are due particular thanks for their help in coordinating our interstate correspondence. It is also my honour to thank Stu Kellaway and Wiṯiyana Marika, who were both with Yothu Yindi at the beginning and contributed greatly to my knowledge of the band.

Numerous people helped this book develop. Djirrimbiḻpiḻwuy Garawirrtja, Rrikawuku Yunupiŋu, Neparrŋa Gumbula and Djaṉgirrawuy Garawirrtja taught me more about Yolŋu languages, law and culture than I could ever have imagined. Yothu Yindi's manager, Alan James, contributed encouragement and support. The band's designer, Trevor van Weeren, sourced archival images. Mary Rudd, Sally Treloyn and Yalmay Marika kindly proofread drafts. And Galarrwuy Yunupiŋu, Scot Morris, Anthony Wallis and Sean Bowden provided wise counsel on rights and permissions.

My research for this book has received generous support from the University of Melbourne, the Australian Institute of Aboriginal and Torres Strait Islander Studies, the Yothu Yindi Foundation, the Australian Research Council and the University of Sydney. I am also very grateful to Ian James of Mushroom Music Publishing and Paul Kelly, represented by Universal Music Publishing, for donating their respective song publishing rights to this project.

I extend warm thanks to Allan Marett for including my work in this series, and to Ross Coleman and his wonderful team at Sydney University Press. Last but not least, I thank the love my life, Melinda Sawers, for her work on our musical scores, and my inspirational colleague, Marcia Langton, for her brilliant epilogue. I could not have completed this book without their encouragement and support.

Aaron Corn, Sydney, 28 January 2009

a note on orthography

My spellings of Yolŋu-Matha words and names in this book follow the orthography most widely recognised by contemporary users of these languages (Zorc 1996; Charles Darwin University 2006). It includes most letters found in the Latin alphabet, but employs additional characters to represent these sounds.

'	is an unvoiced glottal stop
ḏ, ḻ, ṉ, ṯ	are spoken as in English, but with the tongue curled up backwards
dh, nh, th	are spoken as 'd', 'n; and 't' in English, but with the tongue placed flat between the teeth
dj, ny, tj	are equivalent to 'j' in English, 'ni' as in onion, and 'ch' in English
ŋ	represents 'ng' as in ring
rr	represents a rolled 'r'

The Yolŋu languages also include six vowels with the following spellings.

a	short a, like the 'u' in but
ä	long a, like the 'a' in park
i	short i, like the 'i' in pin
e	long i, like the 'ee' in knee
u	short o, like the 'o' in to
o	long o, like the 'o' in womb

As even minor misspellings in Yolŋu-Matha, like the absence of underlining or a glottal stop, can alter meaning completely, I apply this orthography consistently throughout the book. Readers should therefore be aware that the titles of *Birrkuḏa* and *Diṯimurru* were originally misspelt on album covers as '*Birrkuṯa*' and '*Diṯi Murru*'. Likewise, the towns of Miliŋinbi and Ramanginiṉŋ are officially known as 'Milingimbi' and 'Ramingining'.

introduction

I first experienced Yothu Yindi on television in 1991, while studying music as an undergraduate at the Queensland Conservatorium in Brisbane. The band's first hit single, 'Treaty', had unexpectedly risen it to international attention, and its second album, *Tribal Voice*, would dominate the Australian charts for most of 1992. Back then, I knew very little about Indigenous peoples or how hard my nation had worked to curtail their freedoms for most of our shared history. Nor did it occur to me that contemporary Australia could be home to a people like the Yolŋu, who were largely unaware of their subjugation under the Crown until the early 1930s and have striven to maintain their living traditions ever since.

But really, none of that mattered to me at the time. Like many young Australians, I was simply captivated by the vitality and difference of Yothu Yindi's music videos for 'Treaty', 'Djäpana' and 'Tribal Voice'. But then in 1992, came the historic Mabo judgement which overturned the doctrine of *terra nullius*, the legal fiction that Australia had been unoccupied at the time of British settlement in 1788, and led to the passage of the *Native Title Act 1993*. Prime Minister Paul Keating, in his moving Redfern Park Speech of 1992, acknowledged that Australia's nationhood had come at the terrible expense of systemic injustices against Aboriginal and Torres Strait Islander peoples, and urged for Reconciliation. Yothu Yindi's engaging lead singer and songwriter, Mandawuy Yunupiŋu, was quickly recognised as a key advocate of Aboriginal Reconciliation, and on Australia Day 1993, was named Australian of the Year to coincide with the United Nations International Year for the World's Indigenous People.

Like many Australians at that time, I was greatly moved by the symbolism of these developments, but also took to heart the deeper social justice principles expressed by Yothu Yindi in songs such as 'Treaty' and 'Mabo'. I felt compelled to discover as much as possible about the political history of Indigenous engagements in Australia. And so in 1995, I enrolled in a PhD at the University of Melbourne, and commenced work on a project that would eventually become my thesis on popular music in remote Arnhem Land in Australia's Northern Territory.

I met Mandawuy Yunupiŋu on my first field trip to Arnhem Land in 1996. We sat on the porch in the breeze of his modest beachside home at Gunyaŋara, and I asked him fairly open questions about Yothu Yindi's history and politics. In retrospect, I was greatly underprepared for his answers. They stretched far beyond my basic understanding of Indigenous expression, and were steeped in a long continuum of Yolŋu law and cross-cultural engagements of which I knew very little.

When I met Mandawuy again in 1999 at the first Garma Festival of Traditional Culture at Guḻkuḻa, I had done my homework. In the intervening years, I had visited most of the Indigenous communities in Arnhem Land, witnessed traditional ceremonies, participated in community festivals and other music initiatives, interviewed many locals about their life experiences since the 1950s, translated many of their original songs from Yolŋu-Matha, and read extensively on the region's history and many distinct traditions. This time, I was much better equipped to engage with Mandawuy's ideas, and I was awestruck by the depth of Yolŋu tradition that he brought to his work with Yothu Yindi. I also began to appreciate just how central Mandawuy's immediate family had been to the struggle for Indigenous land rights since the early 1960s, and how his direct experiences of state injustice had informed the composition of songs like 'Treaty'.

Conscious of how long it had taken me to unravel this story, I enthusiastically floated the idea of a book that would help others to understand the significance of this extraordinary legacy as reflected in Yothu Yindi's songs. My work on this book commenced in 2001, and through the intervening years of planning, research and consultation, *Reflections & voices* is now a reality. It is a tribute to Yothu Yindi, whose music introduced audiences all over the world to the unique beauty of Yolŋu culture.

But in particular, it is my tribute to Mandawuy Yunupiŋu, who is known to most as an entertainer and cultural ambassador, but had previously gained wide recognition in the Northern Territory as the visionary educator who championed bicultural learning in Indigenous schools. Having made these schools places where Indigenous and European ways of knowing could be legitimately taught side-by-side, he then sang of a world in which Indigenous and non-Indigenous Australians could live together in harmony and in mutual respect for each other's laws and ways of life.

With its signature blend of Indigenous and non-Indigenous musicians, Yolŋu traditions and international popular styles, Yothu Yindi was the realisation of Mandawuy's vision in microcosm. Now that Australia faces the steep challenges of the Northern Territory Intervention into Aboriginal child welfare, which is contentiously exempt from the *Racial Discrimination Act 1975*, it is important for us all to reflect on this vision, and on the decades of hard work that many Indigenous Territorians have dedicated to building viable futures for their communities and their living traditions with exceptionally limited resources.

I can liken this book to a song within the Yolŋu *Manikay* tradition. It starts with this brief 'introduction' where I hum the bare melody. Its greater body is phrased in three subsequent chapters: 'reflections', 'a legacy of hope', and 'voices'. And it ends with a brief 'conclusion' where I reiterate the key themes that were sung. An 'epilogue' by Marcia Langton and 'appendices' follow.

'Reflections' summarises Yothu Yindi's history, achievements, and background in Yolŋu law, culture and politics. These themes are expanded on in 'a legacy of hope', which is an edited transcript of my interview with Mandawuy for the Music and Social Justice Conference at the University of Sydney in 2005. The specific songs discussed in this second chapter are 'Baywara', 'Djäpana', 'Mainstream', 'Tribal Voice', 'Treaty' and 'Gunitjpirr Man'. Finally, 'voices' offers a guide to the music, lyrics, videos and stories behind eight of Yothu Yindi's best known songs, and includes material taken from my interviews with Mandawuy in Melbourne in 2001.

Discussion of each song is deliberately self-contained for ease of access to all relevant information, but builds on topics discussed earlier in 'reflections' and 'a legacy of hope'. All of my references to specific recordings by Yothu Yindi follow a simple album/track format. 'Treaty' (II/2) therefore refers to the second track on the band's second album. I provide a complete listing of tracks on all six Yothu Yindi albums in the 'discography' appendix.

I hope that you enjoy this book and find in it the excitement that I felt when discussing with Mandawuy his vision for Yothu Yindi, the band's deep roots in Yolŋu tradition, and the compelling history of struggle for equality that its music reflects. I hope that it sparks a broad new awareness of Yothu Yindi's genius and the continuing vitality of traditional Indigenous thought and expression in contemporary Australia.

reflections

Maralitja 'Saltwater Crocodile Man', ancestor of the Gumatj Yolŋu (Galarrwuy Yunupiŋu 1991).

mali'yun

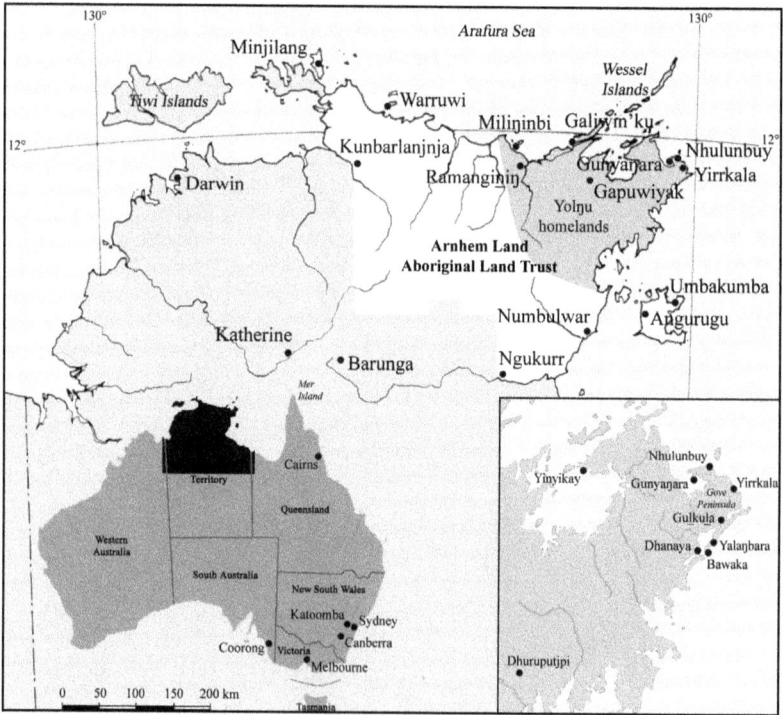

Location of the Yolŋu homelands within Arnhem Land, Australia.

a band with a vision

Yothu Yindi became a household name in Australia in the early 1990s and captivated audiences worldwide with its unprecedented blend of international popular styles and rare Yolŋu traditions from north-east Arnhem Land. Spanning six studio albums, some eighty songs and thirteen music videos (see 'discography'), the band's repertoire draws extensively on hereditary Yolŋu traditions in *Manikay* 'Song' and *Buŋgul* 'Dance'. Individual song items from various traditional *Manikay* series feature prominently on Yothu Yindi's albums. Their usual instrumentation of male voice, the *bilma* 'paired sticks', and *yiḏaki* 'didjeridu' also figure in many of the band's original songs, as do an abundance of themes, lyrics and musical elements drawn directly from the *Manikay* tradition.

Yothu Yindi was formed in Darwin in 1986 by six young musicians from different walks of life. Mandawuy Yunupiŋu (voice, guitar), Wiṯiyana Marika (voice, *bilma*) and Milkayŋu Munuŋgurr (*yiḏaki*) were three Yolŋu men from Yirrkala on the Gove Peninsula, whose families had owned and lived on their sacred homelands in north-east Arnhem Land for countless generations. Mandawuy's work as an executive teacher in Yolŋu schools often took him to Darwin, and this is where he met Stu Kellaway (bass), Cal Williams (guitar) and Andy Beletty (drums) who played together in a band called the Swamp Jockeys. As their friendships grew, they played many early gigs together around Darwin and gained a student following at the Northern Territory University. The Swamp Jockeys backed Mandawuy's growing repertoire of original songs, including 'Djäpana' and 'Mainstream', while the presence of Wiṯiyana and Milkayŋu made it also possible to perform music and dance from traditional *Manikay* and *Buŋgul* repertoire. This balance between original and traditional songs became a key theme of the band's first album, *Homeland Movement* (1989), and remained important in all to follow.

Mandawuy and Stu remained regulars in Yothu Yindi and, over the twenty-one years of its career, were joined by a diverse array of talent. Indigenous musicians included Jodie Cockatoo (voice), Bart Willoughby (drums) from the Adelaide band No Fixed Address, and the young Yolŋu prodigy, Gurrumul Yunupiŋu (voice, guitar, keyboard), who later formed the Saltwater Band and found solo chart success. Two Papuan musicians, Ben Hakalitz (drums) and Buruka Tau-Matagu (keyboard), also worked with Yothu Yindi, as did a variety of famous guests including Peter Garrett from Midnight Oil, the Australian balladeer Paul Kelly, David Bridie from Not Drowning, Waving, Neil Finn from Crowded House, Andrew Farriss from INXS, Liam Ó Maonlaí from the Hothouse Flowers, and Jim Kerr from Simple Minds. Through the prowess of Wiṯiyana Marika and Maŋatjay Yunupiŋu, the band was also renowned for bringing to the stage the dynamism of traditional Yolŋu dance.

Mandawuy Yunupiŋu was born at Yirrkala in 1956, and in 1962, his father, Mungurrawuy, became a leader of the Yolŋu struggle against the mining of bauxite from sacred homelands on the Gove Peninsula. Wiṯiyana Marika's father, Ḏaḏayŋa, was another central

Andy Beletty, Wiṯiyana Marika, Mandawuy Yunupiŋu, Maŋatjay Yunupiŋu and Makuma Yunupiŋu share the stage in an early concert, c1988. Courtesy of Yothu Yindi.

figure in this cause, which consumed a decade of their families' lives and challenged the Australian government to recognise Yolŋu sovereignty. Australia failed this challenge and mining on the Gove Peninsula continues today.

Mandawuy's older brother, Galarrwuy, became involved in this campaign as an interpreter for his elders in the late 1960s. He went on to lobby for the creation of Australia's first land rights bill, the *Aboriginal Land Rights (Northern Territory) Act 1976*, and became responsible for its enforcement when elected Chair of the Northern Land Council in 1977. He was named Australian of the Year for his negotiation of the Ranger uranium mine agreement in 1978. Galarrwuy enthusiastically supported Yothu Yindi from its outset. In 1971, he had released a single of 'Gurindji Blues' by Ted Egan, with a spoken introduction by the great Aboriginal rights activist Vincent Lingiari, and in 1989, contributed one of his own original songs, 'Luku-Wäŋawuy Manikay "Sovereignty Song" 1788', to Yothu Yindi's first album. For later albums, he sang many traditional *Manikay* items and created traditional *Miny'tji* 'Designs' for use as cover art. He is also seen leading a traditional initiation ceremony at Gunyaŋara in the music video for 'Tribal Voice'.

Mandawuy experienced his first rock concert as a teenager at the Sydney Opera House in 1974. He taught himself guitar and later played in a local cover band called the Diamond Dogs at Yirrkala. His career as a composer began at Galiwin'ku in 1983 during his time as Assistant Principal at Shepherdson College. It was there that he was encouraged by Soft Sands, the first Yolŋu band to have toured outside Australia, to compose his first original song, 'Djäpana: Sunset Dreaming' (Corn with Gumbula 2005).

Mandawuy's originality as a songwriter fuelled his revolutionary thoughts on learning, with songs like 'Mainstream' reflecting his commitment to providing Yolŋu children with a balanced bicultural education. He graduated with a Bachelor of Arts in Education from Deakin University in 1987 as one of the first Yolŋu to earn a full academic degree. And in another first, he was promoted to Principal at the Yirrkala Community Education Centre in 1990. He resigned soon after to pursue his career with Yothu Yindi, and following the remarkable success of the band's second album, *Tribal Voice* (1991), was named Australian of the Year for 1992. He spent the following years with Yothu Yindi busily touring the world.

Though formulated in the early 1980s, Mandawuy's innovations in bicultural schooling remain influential to this day, and in 1998 he received an honorary doctorate from the Queensland University of Technology to mark this important contribution. But the balance engendered by biculturalism as Mandawuy saw it—the balance between Yolŋu and Balanda 'European' perspectives—was also central to his greater social project for Yothu Yindi (Yunupiŋu 1994). This kind of balance was constructive. It allowed for different views to be exchanged, laid foundations for mutual respect between different peoples, and created new possibilities for the coexistence of different ways of life. All of which had been absent from official Balanda thinking when mining continued on the Gove Peninsula despite local pleas.

And so with its mixed repertoire of original and traditional songs, Yothu Yindi became a microcosm of the kind of world its founders wanted to live in. A world where people with different cultural backgrounds, languages and skin colours could exchange ideas and ways of doing things to create something new within a framework of equality, understanding and mutual respect. Along the way, its music introduced audiences all over the world to the unique beauty of Yolŋu culture, and challenged Australians to think again about Indigenous rights.

who are the Yolŋu?

The Yolŋu are the 'People' of north-east Arnhem Land. They have owned and inhabited their many *wäŋa* 'homelands' in this region for countless millennia, and maintain an intimate knowledge of the many sacred sites within them. These include sites that are now deep underwater, but are known to have been above sea level some 11,000 years ago (Bowler 1994; Yunupiŋu & Dhamarraṉdji 1997; Buku-

Larrŋgay Mulka Centre 1999). Today, there are major Yolŋu communities in the towns of Miliŋinbi, Yirrkala, Galiwin'ku, Ramanginiŋ, Gapuwiyak and Gunyaŋara, and these are surrounded by many small outstations where Yolŋu families live on remote homelands.

Yolŋu see themselves as the direct descendants of the original *waŋarr* 'ancestors' who named, shaped and populated north-east Arnhem Land, and are said to remain eternally present and sentient in each homeland. Despite radical changes to their lifestyles in recent decades, Yolŋu continue to observe the knowledge and practices given to them by *waŋarr*, and constantly explore new ways to express this *Rom* 'Law' through cultural innovations such as Yothu Yindi and the Garma Festival.

Yolŋu society is an expansive network of more than sixty hereditary *mala* 'groups', often referred to as clans in English, who conventionally pass ownership of their specific homelands from father to child. Though this network, all Yolŋu *mala* are related as *gurruṯu* 'family'. Mandawuy Yunupiŋu, Wiṯiyana Marika and Milkayŋu Munuŋgurr were respectively born into the Gumatj *mala*, the Rirratjiŋu *mala* and the Djapu' *mala*. Each *mala* owns hereditary *Manikay* 'Songs', *Buŋgul* 'Dances' and *Miny'ṯji* 'Designs' for its homelands, and is also said to possess its own *matha* 'tongue', which includes a unique set of sacred *Yäku* 'Names'. All together, there are seven Yolŋu languages which are collectively referred to as Yolŋu-Matha 'People's Tongues'. The distinct *matha* spoken by each Yolŋu *mala* is effectively a dialect of one of these seven languages.

Six of the eight songs translated later in 'voices' include lyrics in Mandawuy's own Gumatj *matha* which is part of the Dhuwal/Dhuwala language. 'Timeless Land', however, incorporates lyrics sung by Wiṯiyana in the Rirratjiŋu *matha*, and Mandawuy sings 'World Turning' in the Gälpu *matha* of his mother's. Both of these *matha* fall within the Dhaŋu/Djaŋu language.

child and mother

Traditionally, *yothu-yindi* describes the prolific bond between 'child and mother', which forms a cornerstone of Yolŋu society. To say that a child and mother are *yothu-yindi* is to acknowledge that all people in Yolŋu society are born into their father's *mala*, yet nonetheless remain children of their mother's *mala* as well. While ownership of country and other property usually passes from father to child, people also inherit important rights and obligations from their mothers.

This convention runs so deep in Yolŋu society that all *mala* are organised under two equal yet distinct constitutions, called Dhuwa and Yirritja. Each *mala* is either Dhuwa or Yirritja, and likewise, each person within each *mala*. Under Yolŋu law, Dhuwa people and Yirritja people must always intermarry. Therefore, each child always has one parent who is Dhuwa, and another who is Yirritja. Mandawuy was born Gumatj like his father, and this is a Yirritja *mala*. His mother, however, was born into the Gälpu *mala* which is Dhuwa. The respective *mala* of Wiṯiyana and Milkayŋu, Rirratjiŋu

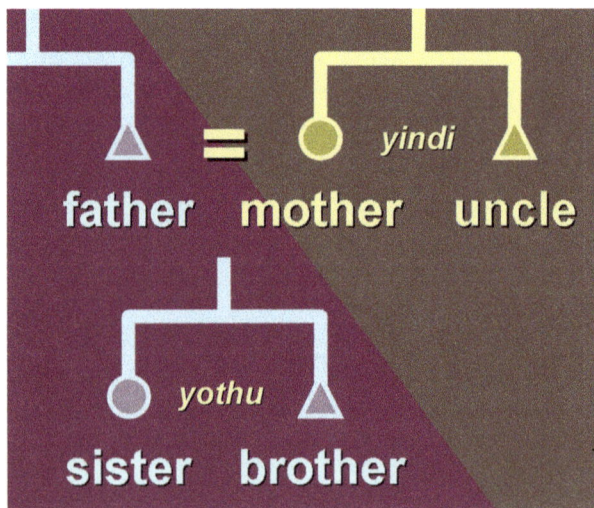

The child-mother relationship is central to Yolŋu society.

and Djapu', are also Dhuwa. Their mothers are Mandawuy's sisters from the Gumatj *mala*, who are therefore Yirritja like him and their father.

Children will always inherit the property of their father's *mala*, but can never own the property of their mother's *mala*, as this is held under a different constitution. Unable to inherit their mother's property, they are free to act in the best interests of her *mala*. They learn and work under her *mala* when young, and as mature adults, act as *djuŋgayi* 'managers' for their mother's *mala* to help make important decisions, settle disputes and conduct ceremonies. In this fundamental way, there is always balance within Yolŋu society. Dhuwa children always look out for their Yirritja mothers, and Yirritja children always look out for their Dhuwa mothers to ensure each other's decisions and actions are legal (Corn & Gumbula 2005). And it is exactly this social balance, equality and interdependence between different bodies of people that the name Yothu Yindi invokes.

Allusions to the *yothu-yindi* 'child-mother' relationships within Mandawuy's own family abound in the band's original songs. 'Mätjala' "Driftwood"' (II/11) sings of the Rirratjiŋu-Gumatj *yothu-yindi* relationship that exists between Wiṯiyana and Mandawuy, his ŋapipi 'mother's brother'. It is reflected again in the two traditional *Manikay* items, one Rirratjiŋu and one Gumatj, that Wiṯiyana quotes in 'Timeless Land' (III/1). Mandawuy alludes to the *yothu-yindi* relationship between his Gumatj daughters and their Rirratjiŋu mother, Yalmay Marika, in 'Mainstream' (I/1, II/8, V/3), and honours his own Gälpu mother in 'Gäpirri "Stingray"' (II/13) and 'Dots on the Shells' (III/13). Such songs capture the mutual respect that exists between Dhuwa and Yirritja in Yolŋu society, and the kind of cross-cultural balance that Yothu Yindi sought to promote in the world beyond.

voices of eternity

Each Yolŋu homeland comes with a unique series of sacred *Yäku* 'Names', *Manikay* 'Songs', *Buŋgul* 'Dances' and *Miny'tji* 'Designs', which like country itself, are passed on through each *mala* as property and as a fundamental expression of *Rom* 'Law'. Together, these hereditary names, songs, dances and designs are known as *Maḏayin* 'Sacred Beauty'. Their many subjects are expressed across all four of these traditional media, and stand as a permanent record of observations made by the original *waŋarr* 'ancestors' as they named, shaped and populated the Yolŋu homelands. They convey an intimate knowledge of each specific homeland, both in terms of its ecological qualities and ceremonial significance.

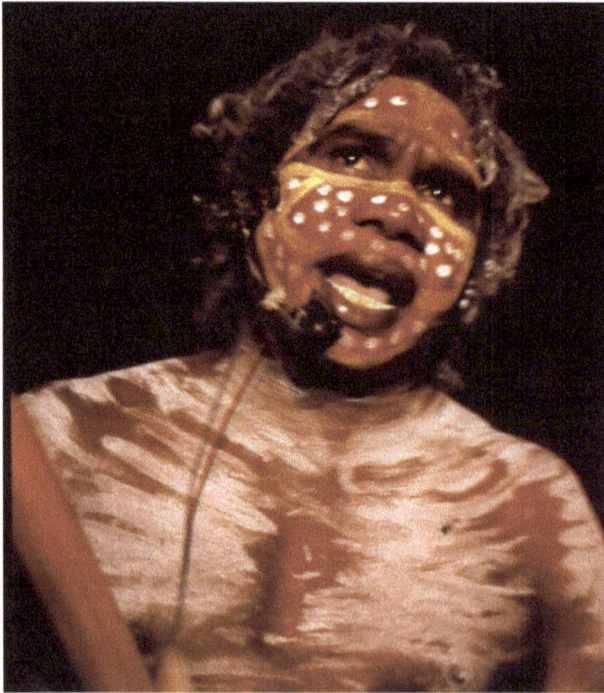

Wiṯiyana Marika sings *Manikay* on stage, c1992.
Courtesy of Yothu Yindi.

Manikay is typically heard in lengthy series of brief songs ordered by subject. It is usually performed by male singers, who wield their own *biḻma* 'paired sticks', and a male *yiḏaki* 'didjeridu' accompanist. It is one of the very few Indigenous musical traditions in Australia to use the didjeridu's overblown hoot as well as the common fundamental drone. The easiest way to identify a *Manikay* series with the particular *mala* that owns it, is by its *ḏämbu* 'head', the melody that is repeated throughout. *Yiḏaki* length and pitch also varies for different *Manikay* series. Yothu Yindi's repertoire mostly draws on *Manikay* series owned by the Gumatj, Rirratjiŋu and Gälpu *mala*.

Manikay lyrics do not tell straightforward stories. They are notoriously cryptic, and make extensive use of each *mala*'s sacred names and archaic words not found in everyday language. The main lyrics of each individual *Manikay* item is called its *makarr* 'thigh', and later in 'voices', I use this term to describe repeated sections in 'Djäpana', 'Treaty', 'Timeless Land' and 'Ghosts Spirits' which are neither verses nor choruses, but direct quotations of traditional songs. Each *Manikay* item has an ABA' structure that comprises A) an unaccompanied hummed introduction, B) the accompanied *makarr* in full, and A') an unaccompanied sung coda. The introduction and coda can be omitted at the singer's discretion. In full ceremony, each *Manikay* item will be accompanied by its corresponding dances, and performers will usually wear various designs drawn from its list of subjects (Corn & Gumbula 2007).

The *Manikay* tradition also extends to the *milkarri* 'crying' songs performed by women, which share the same melodic and lyrical content as men's *Manikay* items (Magowan 2007). It also allows for *yuṯa* 'new' items to be composed for performance in informal contexts (Knopoff 1992). Both of these practices emphasise the stylised expression of *warwu* 'sorrow', which is a key aesthetic within the *Manikay* tradition as a whole.

The more radical extension of traditional *Manikay* subjects into Yothu Yindi's original songs is a hallmark of the compositional style first developed by Mandawuy with 'Djäpana' in 1983. The band's

Takbing Siwaliya from Makassar at the Garma Festival (Jeff Dunn 2005).

fifth album, *One Blood* (1999), offers an interesting insight into this process. On this album, traditional *Manikay* items precede four original songs that then go on to quote them: 'One Blood' (v/ 2), 'Djäpana' (v/8), 'Tears for Law' (v/13) and 'Our Land' (v/ 17).

Another musical tradition performed by Yothu Yindi was *Djaṯpaŋarri*, which was highly popular among youths at Yirrkala between the 1930s and 1970s. In this tradition, young men would gather with *biḻma* and *yiḏaki*, played on the fundamental drone only, and try to outdo each other in the exuberance of their dancing. The songs themselves were composed to reflect everyday life, and were characterised by improvised calls of encouragement to those dancing. 'Gapu "Water"' (II/1), 'Biyarrmak "Comic"' (II/14) and 'Cora [an old supply barge]' (IV/14) exemplify the traditional *Djaṯpaŋarri* style, while 'Treaty' (II/2) directly quotes another *Djaṯpaŋarri* item composed by Rrikin Burarrwaŋa in the early 1950s. He is one of the three Gumatj masters of *Djaṯpaŋarri* to whom *Tribal Voice* is dedicated.

visitors from abroad

Centuries before contact with Balanda Australians, the Yolŋu held extensive relations with other foreign peoples. These included the Maŋgatharra 'Makassans' who sailed annually from the Indonesian port of Makassar on Sulawesi, the Dutch colonists of Indonesia, the mysterious fair-skinned Bayini who predated Makassan contact by hundreds of years (Mountford 1956: 333), and Pacific Islander whalers who Yolŋu called the Wuymu. Fleets of boats from Makassar visited Australia's northern shores between the mid-seventeenth and early twentieth centuries. Their crews collected *trepang* 'sea cucumber' from the warm coastal waters, and also enjoyed the right to harvest turtle shell, pearls and timber. In return, their Yolŋu hosts received imported metal, axes, sugar, tobacco, alcohol, rice and textiles. This valuable arrangement came to an abrupt end in 1906 when the State Government of South Australia, which then administrated the Northern Territory, imposed costly entry tariffs upon all foreign vessels (Macknight 1976).

The legacy of Makassan contact nonetheless endures. The tamarind trees they seeded still grow all along Australia's northern coast, and remnants of their pottery and tools are still found at their former camps. Contemporary Yolŋu-Matha also contains hundreds of Makassan loan words such as *rrupiya* 'money', *bandirra* 'flag', *buthulu* 'bottle', *lipalipa* 'canoe', *dhamburra* 'drum' and *baŋ'kulu* 'axe' (Cooke 1996; Toner 2000). Since 1988, Yolŋu have shared in several reunions with their Makassan neighbours (McIntosh 1996a), and in 2005, Takbing Siwaliya performed traditional Makassan music and dance for their Yolŋu hosts and international guests at the Garma Festival.

Yolŋu histories of ancestral contact with the Makassans, the Bayini and other foreigners also figure prominently in some hereditary repertoires of names, songs, dances and designs. Mandawuy reflects on their importance in 'Makassan Crew' (VI/1), and alludes to the untimely demise of Bayini marauders in 'Djäpana' (I/4).

resistance on the frontier

It was not until the 1870s, more than eight decades after the British claimed Australia at Sydney Cove in 1788, that Balanda first attempted to settle Arnhem Land. Many Aboriginal families would never recover from the decades of bloodshed that came to the region with the intrusion of pastoralists, poachers and police (Mundine 1998). Mandawuy's mother-in-law was one of the few people of the Manatja' *mala* to survive when intruders with guns and horses massacred her family in the first decade of the twentieth century. Yothu Yindi marked this tragedy with the release of its fourth album, *Birrkuda: Wild Honey* (1996).

To compound such tragedies, most early attempts to establish pastoralism in Arnhem Land swiftly failed, and very soon, many settler Australians thought the region to be too remote and inhospitable for European settlement. Following two decades of indecision, the Australian government eventually declared Arnhem Land an Aboriginal Reserve in 1931. In theory, the region's isolation would allow local Aboriginal peoples to pursue their traditional lifestyles unhindered. While the arrival of Christian missionaries stopped most of the pastoral massacres, it posed a new threat to tradition. The first Methodist mission to the Yolŋu was established at Miliŋinbi in 1923, followed by Yirrkala in 1934 and Galiwin'ku in 1942. Fortunately, Yolŋu leaders were quick to negotiate a dialogue with the open-minded Methodists which enabled their own ceremonial traditions to be openly practised alongside Christianity.

Yolŋu leaders took for granted their inherited legal jurisdiction over their homelands until 1934, when Dhäkiyarr Wirrpanda of the Djapu' *mala* was tried in Darwin for the alleged murder of Constable Albert McColl. McColl's police troop had left Darwin in the previous year to find the killers of five Japanese sailors, who in 1932 had committed a string of assaults against Yolŋu while camped on the Djapu' homeland of Dhuruputjpi. While searching for the sailors' killers, McColl made the fatal error of assaulting Dhäkiyarr's wife.

The Supreme Court of the Northern Territory found Dhäkiyarr guilty of McColl's murder and sentenced him to death. A torrent of public outcry from interstate ensued, and so following an appeal to the High Court of Australia, Dhäkiyarr was released. But he would never return home. Dhäkiyarr mysteriously disappeared the night of his release from jail and his body was never found (Read 2005). In 2003, his family led a traditional Yolŋu ceremony into the Supreme Court of the Northern Territory to reconcile with McColl's family and lay Dhäkiyarr's soul to rest with his eternal ancestors (Collins & Murray, 2004).

the struggle for justice

The first direct challenge to Yolŋu sovereignty came in 1962 when the Australian government summarily granted NABALCO the right to mine bauxite on the Gove Peninsula. Leaders of the nine Yolŋu *mala* living at Yirrkala whose homelands would be effected by this decision were quick to protest. They painted two enormous bark panels with their most sacred hereditary designs, one for the Dhuwa *mala* and one for the Yirritja *mala*, which became an unprecedented symbol of their solidarity against the mine. Later known as the Yirrkala Church Panels, they were presented to the mission authority at Yirrkala, and displayed in the local church on either side of the cross. A formal petition to the federal House of Representatives in Canberra followed in 1963 (Attwood & Markus, 1999: 202–03).

Despite this protest, mining started as planned in 1968. The only concession granted the Yolŋu leadership was over the naming of the residential mining town, in response to the Wuyal Petition of 1968. Its original Rirratjiŋu name, Nhulunbuy, was retained and was not replaced with the planned alternative, Gove (Marika 1995: 99–109). Mining destroyed the land, polluted the waters, brought Balanda residents who looked down upon the Yolŋu, and led to the opening of Nhulunbuy's public bar despite legal action taken by staunchly opposed Yolŋu leaders (Dunlop, 1970–96).

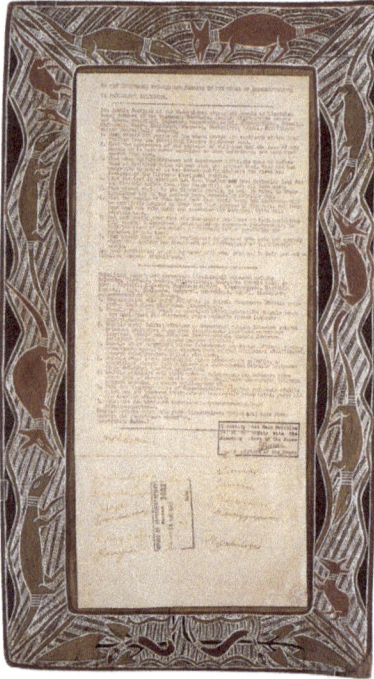

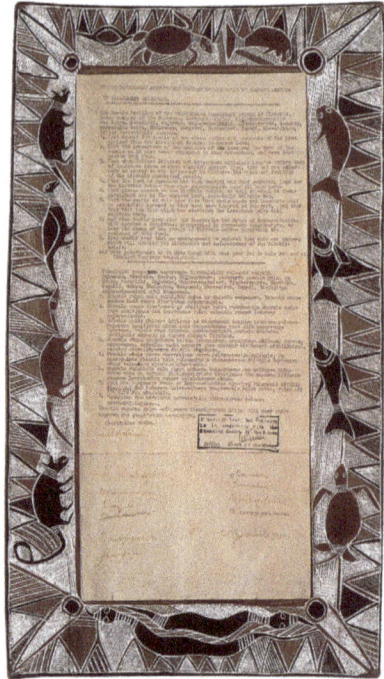

Above: The Yirrkala Petition, 1963. Courtesy of the Australian Parliament House Art Collection.

Left: The Wuyal Petition, 1968.Courtesy of the Australian Parliament House Art Collection.

Galarrwuy Yunupiŋu, Ḏaḏayŋa Marika and Daymbalipu Munuŋgurr outside the Australian Capital Territory Supreme Court in Canberra (Ian Mitchell 1970).

And so in 1968, the Yirrkala leaders, including Mandawuy's father and Wiṯiyana's father, lodged their case against the Australian government and NABALCO with the Supreme Court of the Northern Territory. Mandawuy's older brother, Galarrwuy, interpreted for his elders all through the hearings. The evidence they presented hinged on the innermost restricted proofs of how Yolŋu own their homelands under *Rom* 'Law' by the original *waŋarr* 'ancestors' (Williams 1986). Nonetheless in 1971, their case failed. Justice Blackburn ruled that Yolŋu sovereignty was in no way recognised by the Crown, and had it ever existed, it had ceased when the British claimed possession of Australia at Sydney Cove in 1788 (Supreme Court of the Northern Territory 1971). Galarrwuy later parodied this unwelcome decision in 'Ḻuku-Wäŋawuy Manikay "Sovereignty Song" 1788' (1/14) to mark the bicentennial of Crown occupation in Australia (Corn & Gumbula 2004). Many other Yothu

Yindi songs, such as 'Written on a Bark' (v/9) and 'Gone is the Land' (vi/12), reflect more solemnly on this tragic loss.

A federal commission into Blackburn's ruling followed in 1971, and although government ignored most of its recommendations, it did result in Australia's first land rights bill in 1976. Under this act, Arnhem Land and other Aboriginal areas in the Northern Territory gained recognition as Aboriginal Land Trusts, and Indigenous bodies like the Northern Land Council were established to protect them against unwelcome exploitation.

First elected in 1977, Galarrwuy was still Chair of the Northern Land Council in 1988, when he and Wenten Rubuntja of the Central Land Council called on Prime Minister Robert Hawke to negotiate a Treaty with the Indigenous peoples of Australia. This call took the form of the Barunga Statement, which they presented to Hawke at an Indigenous community event near Katherine called the Barunga Sport and Cultural Festival. Its logic was simple. Indigenous Australians had never formally ceded their sovereignty to the Crown, so a Treaty was required to rectify this situation. In return, Indigenous peoples wanted recognition of their continuing freedom and rights as Australia's original owners (Attwood & Markus, 1999: 316–17). Hawke responded with a tearful promise of swift positive action that would never come to pass. And so in 1990, when the issue had all but faded from public memory, Yothu Yindi collaborated with Peter Garrett and Paul Kelly to send a timely reminder and create its most famous and enduring song, 'Treaty' (ii/2).

Today, the original Yirrkala Petition, the Wuyal Petition and the Barunga Statement all hang in the Australian Parliament House in Canberra on permanent public display, as constant reminders of missed opportunities to redress past injustices. Yet still, Yolŋu live in hope that their self-evident rights as the owners of north-east Arnhem Land will one day be fully recognised by the Crown through constitutional reform. Only last year in 2008, Galarrwuy presented Prime Minister Kevin Rudd with a new Yirrkala Petition calling for new leadership on this front (Yunupiŋu 2008). It remains to be seen

Witiyana dances for his mother's *mala*, the Gumatj, at the 2004 Garma Festival.
Courtesy of the Yothu Yindi Foundation.

if Rudd's government, which includes former rock star Peter Garrett as Minister for the Environment, Heritage and the Arts, will move Australia forward in this cause.

hope for the future

In 2004, Mandawuy flew to Sydney for the Deadlys, where he received the Jimmy Little Award for Lifetime Achievement in Aboriginal and Torres Strait Islander Music. But by then, his long years of touring and his long battle with kidney disease were exacting a harsh toll. Tragedy struck with the unexpected death of Yothu Yindi's co-founder, Milkayŋu Munuŋgurr, in 2007. And so in 2008, with Mandawuy's own health rapidly deteriorating, Yothu Yindi played its final concert in Darwin. The band is remembered for its introduction of Yolŋu culture to audiences worldwide, and its bold reminder of the Treaty promised by Prime Minster Hawke in 1988.

However, stemming from Mandawuy's revolutionary work as an educator, Yothu Yindi's social contributions always extended far beyond music. In 1990, the band established the Yothu Yindi Foundation to promote maintenance of tradition and economic development in Yolŋu communities. Its initiatives have included the Yirrŋa Music Development Centre, which opened at Gunyaŋara in 1999 as a venue for Indigenous music workshops, and the feature film *Yolŋu Boy* (Johnson, dir. 2000) on which Mandawuy and Galarrwuy worked as associate producers (Corn 2007). The foundation has also recorded the Contemporary Masters Series (2001–03), a collection of six albums featuring traditional music performed by celebrated ceremonial leaders including Galarrwuy Yunupiŋu and Djalu Gurruwiwi (Skinnyfish Music 2009).

Each year, the Yothu Yindi Foundation hosts the Garma Festival of Traditional Culture at Guḻkuḻa. Named *garma* 'public', after the Yolŋu-Matha term describing all traditional knowledge that can be openly shared, the Garma Festival continues to realise Yothu Yindi's vision for sharing Yolŋu culture with people from all over the world (Yothu Yindi Foundation 2006). Highlights of this event include stunning displays of traditional music and dance by Indigenous performers from throughout northern Australia, concerts by Yolŋu bands, and appearances by visiting Indigenous performers including the Bauls of Bengal in 2004 and Takbing Siwaliya from Sulawesi, Indonesia in 2005.

The festival also hosts an annual Key Forum which has addressed Indigenous issues in education, health, law, art, leadership, tourism and the environment. And from 2002 to 2006, it was the venue of the Symposium on Indigenous Music and Dance, the annual meeting of the National Recording Project for Indigenous Performance in Australia (Corn, 2007). Mandawuy was a leading Indigenous founder of this important initiative, and launched it at the Garma Festival in 2004.

For two decades, Yothu Yindi enthralled audiences worldwide. Its music has captivated millions with its unique dynamism, and has offered a rare glimpse into an Indigenous culture that continues to flourish in Australia despite the mining of its homelands and the Australian government's failure to prevent this. Yothu Yindi's innovations, both musical and social, express the continuity of contemporary Yolŋu communities with the *Rom* 'Law' of their original ancestors, while simultaneously using this sacred inheritance to encourage respectful coexistence between Indigenous and non-Indigenous Australians and their respective ways of life. This is the deeper story of Yothu Yindi's genius that is yet to be told.

a legacy of hope

A sacred Gumatj ŋathu 'cycad' palm (Galarrwuy Yunupiŋu 1991).

from a keynote interview hosted by
Aaron Corn (AC) with Mandawuy Yunupiŋu (MY)
for the Musicological Society of Australia
at the Music and Social Justice Conference in Sydney,
28 September 2005

Selected homelands owned by different *mala* to which Mandawuy relates as:

● own countries	Gumatj
● mother country	Gälpu
● mother's mother country	Dhaḻwaŋu
● sister's child countries	Rirratjiŋu
● sister country	Wangurri

AC Mandawuy, welcome back to Sydney for this special conference on music and social justice. You've enjoyed a distinguished career as one of Australia's foremost cultural ambassadors. How did music become such an enormous part of your life?

MY Well, you know Aaron that music is integral to Yolŋu life where I come from up in Arnhem Land. When Yolŋu are born, they carry that special gift, especially males, who have music running in their blood. So when a person is born, they are automatically exposed to music. I grew up at Yirrkala where there were only a handful of white missionaries, so my exposure to song and dance was immense where I come from.

AC Social justice themes spanning a whole range of issues including land rights, Indigenous sovereignties, religious freedom, race relations and, of course, cultural survival are found throughout Yothu Yindi's repertoire. When did you first become aware that you could use music as a means of educating people about the social justice concerns of Indigenous Australians?

MY I think that, in a contemporary way of looking at it, my exposure to the Western way in the classroom, learning Western types of music and adjusting to them, and getting to know the meanings behind them was a task in its own. I think that was the drive that made me want to switch it all around and use my Yolŋu thinking to combine the Western way with the Yolŋu way so that others might understand Yolŋu perspectives. I think that was my objective.

AC You mentioned your homelands in north-east Arnhem Land, and there are some sixty Yolŋu hereditary groups who own countries here. Many of the towns in this area were founded as Methodist missions in the early part of the twentieth century. So Mandawuy, you were born in 1956 at the Yirrkala Mission, which the Methodists founded in 1934. What was it like growing up in that environment? You said there were only a handful of Methodist missionaries at Yirrkala so what was that like for you as a child?

MY Well I grew up in a semi-nomadic lifestyle, and when I wasn't going to school, my father and mother would take me out and go hunting, following the seasons of course, so there was that balance in my education. My mother taught me all the things that I should know about, all the types of things that were in season on the land, and my father taught me things that were in season too, especially the big game. So I had balance in learning how to follow the seasons and going to school as well. There was a big push for me to pick up academic skills, as well as being exposed to and knowing the Western way.

AC There was quite an exclusive selective high school near Yirrkala called Dhupuma College, wasn't there?

MY Yeah.

AC And people were hand picked to go to that school.

MY That's right, yeah.

AC So what did Dhupuma offer?

MY Dhupuma was a residential secondary school where a mixture of people from Arnhem Land and the Gulf of Carpentaria came. This is where they rubbed shoulders with local Yolŋu peers, and tried to pick up on secondary education. But of course in 1981, it was closed by the Northern Territory Government.

AC Why do you think it was closed?

MY Well I think the Northern Territory Government didn't want black people to be smart.

AC And therein lies our first social justice issue. So spread throughout north-east Arnhem Land are many homelands to which you hold very personal and spiritual relationships, either as a Gumatj owner through your father's lineage, or as a descendant of other Yolŋu groups through your mother's lineage. On our map, I've colour coded them so that red represents your own Gumatj wäŋa-ŋaraka 'bone countries'. Orange represents the homelands owned by your Gälpu ŋändipulu 'mother's group', and so on. Yellow is your Dhaḻwaŋu märipulu 'mother's mother's group', green is your Rirratjiŋu wakupulu 'sister's child's group', and blue is your Wangurri yapapulu 'sister group'. Can you describe the kind of relationship you have to your own Gumatj countries, and how that differs from kinds of relationships you have with your mother's countries and your mother's mother's country, because references to these places and their law crop up again and again in your repertoire?

MY Okay, well you need to understand the *yothu-yindi* or 'child-mother' structure. *Yothu-yindi* is a structure that all Yolŋu recognise, and in this worldview everyone is either Dhuwa or Yirritja.

AC Your two constitutions.

MY Yeah, both are equal, parallel and balanced, and everybody has a responsibility to both. So I'm responsible to my father's group which is Yirritja, and I have an extra responsibility to my mother's group which is Dhuwa. I'm an owner in Gumatj country and law. But I am like a manager or a *djuŋgayi* to my mother's country and law, and to her Gälpu songs and dances. You can see it in ceremonies when *djuŋgayi* manage their mother's law. Likewise, a Dhuwa person born from my sisters, they have extra responsibilities to our side.

AC You can potentially inherit from your mother's mother group as well, because once you skip a generation along the mother's line, you're under the same constitution again.

MY That's right. That's the mother's mother. It's the *gutharra-märi* 'mother's mother-daughter's child' relationship, and that is an important and powerful way to pass responsibility to the next generation.

AC So really, this system provides a comprehensive set of checks and balances between different Yolŋu groups who might otherwise compete for country and resources.

MY Well you know, it's just one of those things that Yolŋu have had since day one. We came up with a very acute way of seeing the world, and how things should be shared equally within society without making a federal case out of it.

AC Speaking of which, 'Baywara', the song named after your mother's Olive Python ancestor, beautifully describes the concepts that underpin Yolŋu sovereignty. How did you come to compose 'Baywara'?

MY This is a special song. In 1991, my uncle D̲adayŋa Marika, who is considered to be the father of land rights, passed away. We were recording our second album, *Tribal Voice*, at that time, and when he passed away, we were in a mobile studio at Gunyaŋara. We were sitting outside that evening when he passed away, and we could see lightning talking over the sea and over the freshwater.

AC Wow.

MY These two snakes were talking to each other in the freshwater and the saltwater, and that inspired me to write this song about *Baywara*. D̲adayŋa was a master of that philosophy and he taught a lot of the ways that Yolŋu are initiated through it.

AC Wonderful, so the song's chorus describes *Baywara* as 'Maker of the Land, Maker of the Song, Maker of the Constitution'. As a Yolŋu intellectual, how do you understand the relationships between those three entities: land, song and constitution?

MY It's all integral, all one. You can't isolate one from the other. It's all interwoven very tightly and immovably. That is written in our bark paintings, on our log coffins which are like giant scrolls, and in the many songs sung in any of Arnhem Land's languages. Everyone recognises this. Even down in central Australia where they sing with boomerangs, they talk about the same thing. It's the law. It's the basis from where we come.

AC Okay, so through your father's line, as a descendant of the original Gumatj ancestors, you inherit a whole range of different hereditary property that is passed on to the members of your *mala*. You inherit *wäŋa* 'country'. You inherit *Rom* 'Law', and then you have the protocols needed to practice *Rom* correctly and follow the footsteps of ancestors. So you also inherit your *Ma̲dayin*: all those sacred canons of *Yäku* 'Names', *Manikay* 'Songs', *Buŋgul* 'Dances' and *Miny'tji* 'Designs', all of which you draw on in Yothu Yindi's creative work. It's becoming clear that under this system music and dance are quite central to the execution of legal processes concerning country, people and their decisions in life. But there also seems to be an immutable spiritual relationship with ancestors that Yolŋu maintain throughout their lives by following *Rom* and practicing their *Maḏayin*. How would you describe your own relationship with ancestors, including the people you've known in life, through your own practice as a musician and dancer?

MY Yeah, if you ever see people dancing at a big ceremony, whether they be Shark people or Stingray people ... At that funeral at Dhanaya, you saw my family and me dancing *Bäru* 'Saltwater Crocodile', the Maralitja man. *Bäru* is another name for Maralitja. Maralitja discovered fire in the beginning. So when you're dancing *Bäru*, you become. You're transformed into Maralitja. And that's when you say, when talking to the people, that 'I'm the Maralitja. I own the land. I own that philosophy. I own that knowledge. I hold copyright over that land and you can't take that away from me.' The other *mala* are the same. When the Shark people are doing their Shark dance, they're transformed into the Shark man ancestor. So that's how one becomes transformed into something they want to show, they want to tell, in that most classical way. The classical way of making your point be known is by doing it in unity and strength with your *mala*. And of course, the *yothu-yindi* balance is always there in that strength and unity.

AC Having performed in *Buŋgul* myself over the past years, I've often had the feeling that, every time somebody sings *Manikay* or dances *Buŋgul*, they're contributing to the maintenance of sovereign relationships to country in Australia that clearly predate the British Crown. Do you think that many Yolŋu would agree with that position?

MY Very much so, many people would agree with that because we're still practising our law. We're still doing it regardless of our laws being rejected or being trivialised by mainstream Australian law. We don't care. We keep going because it's important to pass our law on to the next generation. It strengthens our identity as Aboriginal people, the First Nations of this country.

AC Let's go back to your very first song, 'Djäpana: Sunset Dreaming', which you composed in 1983 while you were working as Assistant Principal at Shepherdson College in Galiwin'ku on Elcho Island. 'Djäpana' was composed a few years before the formation of Yothu Yindi in 1986, so where did the idea for this song come from? How did the idea to put music together in this way come to you?

MY Well, this is what happened. It was my first attempt and I had to start somewhere. So one evening after work, I was sitting with a friend of mine. I had a guitar and I was feeling sad for my family. My family didn't come with me at that time. They came afterwards, maybe two months after I was there at Galiwin'ku on my own. But I was sitting, I was thinking, I was worrying about my family, and it was sundown. I was thinking about the lines in the traditional *djäpana Manikay*. I was thinking '*warwu* "sorrow"'. I was thinking '*djäpana, rräma rrämani, dhurulaŋala galaŋgarri* "coral sunset, coral sunset clouds, fading coral sunset"'. I was thinking about all those names that make one sad and about my family, because *djäpana* is about thinking back to your family. So my instinct was to grab the guitar. Also at that time, there was a big movement in which most of the local Yolŋu bands were into gospel songs. So my objective was to say, 'Now listen guys, there are other avenues. Think about your culture.' My struggle was to preserve my culture, and the way that I wanted to do that was to write a song with all the modern Western elements, but also with lines and lyrics that described what I was thinking in the traditional way.

AC Being one of the first people to draw on *Maḏayin* in a popular way, how did people at Galiwin'ku take this at the time?

MY Well, the next day after composing 'Djäpana', I just went to the old band called Soft Sands and I asked them if they could play my song using their equipment. So I was able to feel it with the drums and the bass guitar, and the lead and rhythm guitars. I then worked out the chorus lines as time went on, and started to give it a

Mutitjpuy Munuŋgurr teaches *mäṉda* 'octopus' choreography against a *djäpana* sunset, and Mandawuy dances *djäpana* with a *mäṉda* design painted on his front in 'Djäpana' (Yothu Yindi 1991).

contemporary rock'n'roll feel but still maintained that Yolŋu side to it.

AC Okay, so some of the things that are related to the *djäpana* subject, the coral sunset, are things like *mäṉda* 'octopus'.

MY Yep.

AC And we can see an octopus dance and design here in the 'Djäpana' video clip from 1991. But primarily, the kind of *Manikay* series that *djäpana* is drawn from is really about pre-British foreign contact, isn't it?

MY Yep.

AC This kind of series is primarily a Yolŋu means of documenting contact with a whole range of foreign peoples before British occupation in the 1920s.

MY Like the Makassans.

AC Yeah, peoples like the Makassans from Sulawesi, earlier Bayini visitors, whalers like the Wuymu from Austronesia, the Dhuthurru who were the Japanese, and also Balanda 'European' mariners who started with the Dutch. There's not a lot in this Yolŋu history to suggest that the British First Fleet could have rightfully claimed sovereignty over the entire Australian continent when it landed here in Sydney in 1788. Yolŋu had such extensive relationships with other visiting peoples for so long.

MY Well, that's part of our knowledge now, part of the library in our minds and in our paintings. We included those that came without indoctrinating us into their way or claiming our land. Out of respect for them, we made them part of our culture, our knowledge, and our songs and dances. So *Djäpana* therefore ends the song series. It might take all day, and then at the end, *djäpana* is about saying goodbye basically. Saying goodbye to the day and to the people.

A Dhalwaŋu hollow log coffin painted with anchor, octopus and coral sunset designs against a *djäpana* sunset at Gurrumuru (Aaron Corn 2005).

AC From wherever they come?

MY Yeah, from wherever they come.

AC There are some quite interesting stories of Bayini contact at Bawaka, the Gumatj homeland where 'Djäpana' is grounded, and also of Balanda contact at your mother's mother's country, Gurrumuru. Could you just tell us a little about those two countries please?

MY Yeah, Gurrumuru was the place on Buckingham Bay where the Balanda came. Matthew Flinders came and anchored there, and therefore the anchor is very significant there. The rope and the chain are also significant. Therefore, when we sing *Manikay* from Gurrumuru, we sing about the Balanda coming to that land. On the other side of the bay is a country called Garrthalala, and here, the Dutch came. But before them, the Bayini visitors came just like at Bawaka. So there, we sing about the sword and the anchor, the chain and the rope, and the mast of the Bayini ship. So that's very important.

AC In the mid-1980s, traditional Yolŋu models for fair exchange between different peoples, whether they be members of different hereditary groups or peoples from elsewhere, became central to your work as Assistant Principal at Shepherdson College. And soon after that, to your work as Principal of the school at Yirrkala. In your Boyer Lecture from 1993, you describe having always been challenged by the underlying ideology of assimilation that permeated the classrooms in which you yourself were schooled, and wanting to change this through your own work as an educator. How did you go about instigating this change and how did your third song, 'Mainstream', fit into that?

MY Yeah, this was my first challenge to mainstream education. There I was in 1986, for the first time sitting equally with third year students in the university system. There were only five of us from Arnhem Land in the nation sitting at this level and 'Mainstream' became my way of saying, 'Listen, I can come in, I can sit, I can learn, but still, I have my own traditions which are equal to yours.'

AC So 'Mainstream' is not a song about Yolŋu being absorbed into mainstream Australia?

MY No, this is not about assimilation. It's a song about Yolŋu having our own mainstream, our own *Rom* which is equal to yours. This is what I'm talking about in this song.

AC You actually wrote this song as an assignment, didn't you?

MY That's right, yeah. I was going to Deakin University when I wrote 'Mainstream' and it was part of an assignment.

AC It was awarded a High Distinction.

MY That's right, I got an A plus.

AC And of course, the six pretty girls in the first verse are your daughters.

MY That's right. They're my daughters. While you're away studying, you miss your family, so I was thinking about them when I was writing 'Mainstream'.

AC And about their futures and educational possibilities too?

MY Yep, and suddenly two of them are following my footsteps. They've both written songs and are in the school band at Yirrkala, so I'm really proud of them.

AC That's fantastic. So there are two traditional Yolŋu models for balance and equality between different groups or different peoples that come to light in 'Mainstream'. The first is the *yothu-yindi* 'child-mother' relationship from which your band takes its name. In this instance, it refers to your daughters, who are Gumatj through your line, and your wife, who is their Rirratjiŋu mother.

MY Yep.

AC The second model is the *gaṉma* 'converging currents' ideology which is about the meeting of sister groups of equal social standing within Yolŋu society. The metaphor you use for that is the meeting of saltwater and freshwater currents, and the creation of brackish water and *djikuṉguṉ* 'yellow foam' on the surface where they meet. This painting here by your wife, Yalmay Marika, shows Gumatj waters and Wangurri waters, and the black line bordered by yellow

Gaṉma (Yalmay Marika 1989).

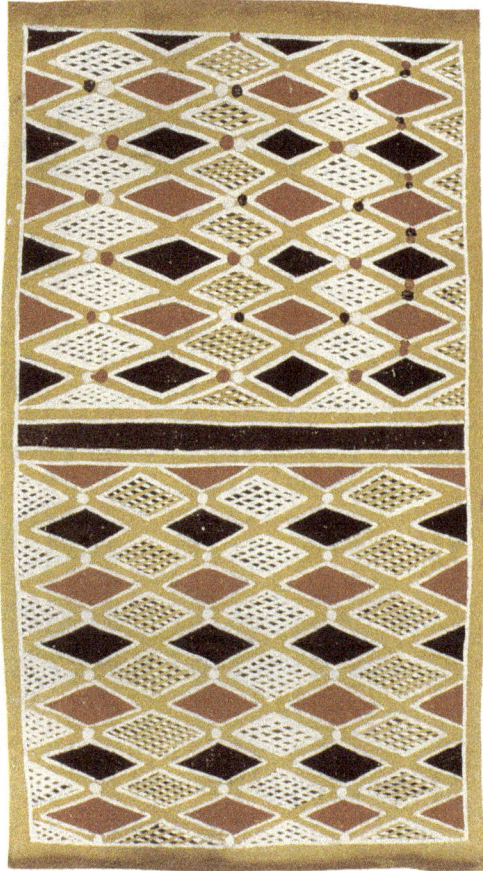

in between them represents the lines of *djikuṉguṉ* on the surface where they meet. Could you talk us through the importance of *gaṉma* in particular, as this is a new concept that we're introducing now.

MY Yeah, *gaṉma* is a place where the water empties out. There's no water, and at that *gaṉma* point, is where fire is symbolised by the seaweed growing there. It's considered a symbol of the fire. And where the dugong eats the seaweed and rolls on it, that's called *gaṉma. Gaṉma* also connects my Gumatj *mala* to the Wangurri *mala*, my *yapapulu* 'sister group'. We have the right to crossover between Gumatj and Wangurri philosophies as my father's father, Yunupiŋu ...

AC The great leader, Yunupiŋu.

MY Yeah, he was the man in charge of that. So in the beginning, there was a crossover where he had responsibilities for Gumatj and responsibilities for Wangurri.

AC In the song, by the time you get the third verse and coda, you have projected these models onto a vision for improving race relations in Australia as well. Do you find that metaphors and models drawn from Yolŋu tradition are equally as adaptable and meaningful when brought to bare on other societies?

MY You know, I think these are drawn from the very depth of our knowledge and the practices that we consider as ritual between the Yolŋu *mala*. Here I'll talk about the Wangurri and the Gumatj as an example so that people don't get confused. There's so direct a parallel between our two aspects of knowledge and the metaphors that we carry to describe things. What might be described in Wangurri, even though you're talking in a different dialect, can be described in Gumatj with the same equal weight carried and the same result at the end of the line.

AC So many good things have come out of Yothu Yindi. You left teaching in the early 1990s to focus more on working with the band. But around the same time, you also instituted the Yothu Yindi Foundation, which launched the Garma Festival of Traditional Culture in 1999. You opened the Yirrŋa Studio to support local musical talent in the same year, and supported production of the feature film, *Yolŋu Boy*, which was released in 2000. There was the Ŋärra' Legal Forum on Australian constitutional law at the 2001 Garma Festival, which was an amazing triumph in its own right, and at the 2004 festival, we launched the National Recording Project for Indigenous Performance in Australia. We've had international guests visit the festival, including this year's reunion with Makassan musicians and dancers, and there's an annual Buŋgul Prize to stimulate interest in ceremonial practice

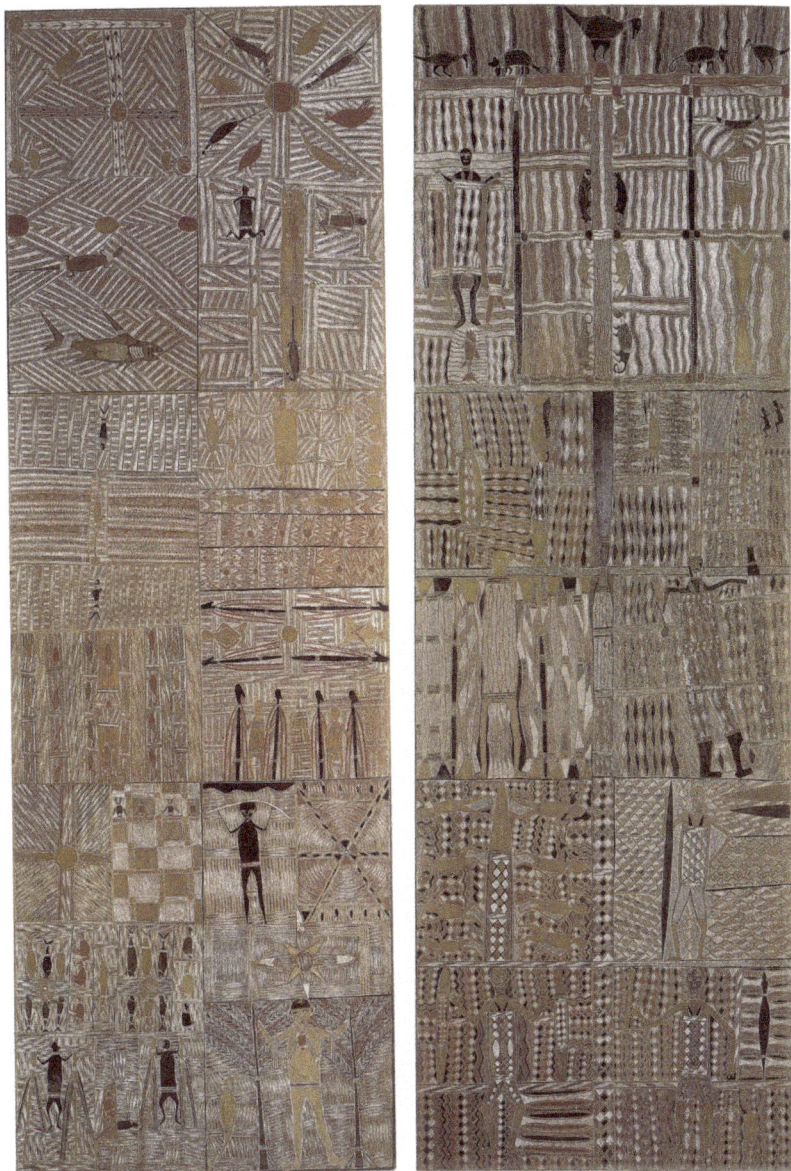

The Yirrkala Church Panels, 1962. Mandawuy's father, Muŋgurrawuy,
painted the designs on the third row from the bottom on the right hand panel.
Courtesy of the Buku-Larrŋgay Mulka Centre.

particularly among children. Any one of these things on its own would be a triumph, and yet when you look at this amazing set of achievements, it must feel absolutely wonderful for you.

MY Very, and it's all due to my elders. Basically, I give credit to them because of their drive, and their recognition of my work and music. This is how I've been able to spread my vision around Australia and indeed the world. With that credibility, I've then been able to bring it back down into the embrace of the Yolŋu in my local community, and give our younger generation a sense of direction and objectives to achieve, whether they be skills for work or music. The Garma Festival was created for that purpose, so it gives the next generation a sense of direction, and makes them feel they're protected by an umbrella where knowledge is an aspect of learning, so they can learn without being forcefully taught.

AC So does this work on your bicultural model?

MY That's right. If they don't achieve anything, there's a fallback situation. They go back to the Garma Festival and say, 'Okay, maybe I'll start again and re-assess.' So that opportunity is there for them.

AC In 1962, Yolŋu leaders at Yirrkala including your father, Mangurrawuy, embarked on a struggle for land justice that would consume an entire decade of their lives and permanently change your family's way of life in particular. News had indirectly reached them of a government plan to mine bauxite from your homelands on the Gove Peninsula, at Galupa near Gunyaŋara, and establish a mining town on Rirratjiŋu country at Nhulunbuy. And their first act was to paint two enormous barks with the most sacred, and indeed restricted, designs of all the local *mala*. They were presented to the local church authority in a demonstration of solidarity against the bauxite mine, and your father painted some of the panels on the right. What do you think the creation of this extraordinary document meant to him?

MY Well, because of his kindness, he was accepting of the ways that non-Aboriginal people came to him. Because he was a leader, he also wanted to bring his law into the church, and I think I inherited from him this thing called balance. He wanted to give non-Aboriginal people, let alone missionaries, a sense of 'Hey listen, we've been here long and we know this. This is just our way of telling you that we go deeper, and our layers of knowledge go deeper than you thought.' The painting that he did on the right is a painting of the Saltwater Crocodile, the Maralitja man. And next to that one, is the Yellow Ochre Man, Wirrili, from the same land at Biranybirany where the crocodile discovered fire. He used my hair for that painting so it's very significant.

AC Quite literally there's a little bit of you in that painting, isn't there?

MY It's historic for me.

AC The Church Panels have always struck me as a symbol of Yolŋu religious freedom. Even though people like your father established a theological dialogue with a benevolent Methodist Church at Yirrkala, their sense of being spiritually-grounded in ancestral law never ceased, and this was part of your own thinking when you composed 'Tribal Voice' at Christmas in 1990, wasn't it? So how did 'Tribal Voice' come about, and how does it reflect the challenges to religious freedom that Yolŋu still face even today?

MY Well it was like I said earlier, people were into the church. It was pretty strong so this was just my way of rejecting it. The whole place was saturated with evangelism, and it seemed there was no way out. It was like every second man and his dog was into it. So my way of

The 'sand dune of love' on the Rirratjiŋu country of Yalaŋbara (Aaron Corn 2005). The sacred *Mawalan* staff that Mandawuy has superimposed here was sent to Canberra by Wandjuk Marika during the Yirrkala land rights struggle in 1972. Courtesy of the Australian Parliament House Art Collection.

challenging this in a nice way without making people go haywire was to say, 'Hey, your tribal voice is going to be here forever. So listen, how about coming down to earth and thinking about where your feet are entrenched, where your reality lies. I've searched for it and I've found it.' So that song, 'Tribal Voice', is about my struggle for recognition of religious freedom, and of course, freedom of speech.

AC *'Yaka menguŋa nhuŋuway Rom. Dhuwala buŋgul gakal ga ḻikan.* "Don't forget your Law. This sacred dance and branch."' This is exactly what you're doing in the 'Tribal Voice' music video, isn't it? You're at a real family initiation ceremony, performing a quite sacred dance that represents your specific branch of ancestry, and holding a similarly sacred *bathi* 'basket'.

MY That's mine, and I'm performing *Gäpirri* 'Stingray'.

AC So to return to the Church Panels, on their heels followed a series of events that were unprecedented in Australian political history. The Yirrkala elders, once again including your father, sent a petition to the Australian House of Representatives calling for the mine to be cancelled. When this went unanswered, the slightly more successful Wuyal Petition of 1968 was sent to the same House asking that Nhulunbuy not be renamed Gove after a US pilot from World War II. This was a direct affront to Rirratjiŋu sovereignty over Nhulunbuy through direct ancestry from Wuyal, the ancestor depicted in this petition. Mining commenced in that same year nonetheless, so your father and his fellow leaders took NABALCO, the company who held the mining lease, and the Commonwealth of Australia to court in the hope of winning an injunction. However, Justice Blackburn ultimately found that Yolŋu sovereignty could not, in any way, be recognised under Australian Crown Law, and that the Yolŋu relationship with their homelands was not proprietary in nature. He further questioned whether Yolŋu plaintiffs in the case were the true descendants of those who might have owned the mine site when the British claimed possession of Australia in 1788. The evidence your father and his contemporaries gave in those hearings included the most deeply restricted details of

Yolŋu law. So after all that effort, how did your father feel after this defeat?

MY I remember that time when he gathered all the elders and they went out bush. They prepared for weeks before flying to Darwin all the things one would want to think about in terms of law. These elders were serious about talking to the judge because they knew that they had to convince the Northern Territory Supreme Court. So they spent maybe two weeks, in the bush doing what elders would do to initiate young men. In this case, they were preparing things to show Blackburn, and they took those things to court. And what did Blackburn do? That was the Supreme Court's biggest stuff up. Further down the line, what happened? In the first Mabo native title case, we saw the same result. So my father was devastated when we lost that court case, and I saw most of the elders alongside with my father saddened. We'll never forget how those aspects of our law, our strength, and our unity were not seen as part of the Australian culture and the Australian way of life in the Yolŋu way.

AC Some comparatively good things eventually came out of this struggle. The first piece of land rights legislation in Australia, the *Aboriginal Land Rights (Northern Territory) Act 1976*, was instituted. Arnhem Land ceased to be an Aboriginal Reserve and under the new act became an Aboriginal Land Trust in which hereditary owners hold inalienable freehold title. This has problems, but it's the best people have under the current system. The Northern Land Council was also set up under the Act to monitor access to Indigenous lands, and your brother, Galarrwuy, soon became its Chair. And in 1988, Galarrwuy took the opportunity to mount a joint Northern Land Council and Central Land Council bid to redress the failure of the Yirrkala case against the mine, and they did this in the form of the Barunga Statement. As most will remember, the state celebrated 1988 as the bicentenary of the Crown in Australia. And in that year, Prime Minister Robert Hawke attended a festival in the small Indigenous community of Barunga just south-east of Katherine. It was there at this Barunga Festival that Galarrwuy and Wenten Rubuntja from the Central

Land Council presented Hawke with the Barunga Statement, and its call for a Treaty between the Indigenous peoples of Australia and the Commonwealth. You should perhaps tell us the story of how Hawke responded to the Barunga Statement, what happened afterwards, and how that ties in to Yothu Yindi's career.

MY In 1986, Yothu Yindi was just formed, and 1988 was when Prime Minister Hawke came up to Barunga. And at that Barunga Festival, he made a statement. He said, 'There shall be a Treaty between Aboriginal Australia and White Australia.' Everyone was really excited about it: 'Ah yeah, finally there'll be a Treaty.' Further down the track, 1988, 1989 and 1990 passed by, and that's when I started to get suspicious about this Treaty. There was no action being taken. So I teamed up with Paul Kelly, Peter Garrett, Bart Willoughby and a few other musicians from Australia, and we wrote that song 'Treaty'. That song is a reflection on the Australian Government at that time and the Australian people for that matter I would think. When is the Treaty? What is the Treaty? How is it going to take form, and in what shape will it come into being in Australia? That's why I wrote that song 'Treaty' as a kind reminder to us all.

AC Finally Mandawuy, there are so many songs in your repertoire that stem from this period of history around the mine.

MY Yep.

AC 'Written on a Bark', 'Gone is the Land', 'Mabo', 'Luku-Wäŋawuy Manikay 1788', 'Lonely Tree' ... But the one you wanted to play for us today is 'Gunitjpirr Man'. Once again, this song was written for Dadayŋa Marika, who stood with a much younger Galarrwuy on the steps of the Australian Capital Territory Supreme Court in Canberra for hearings of the Yirrkala case against the mine. It was composed after his death just like 'Baywara'.

MY This is a song about Yalaŋbara. Yalaŋbara is the sand dune of love. This is where the first Yolŋu child was born, and from there, we were populated. So this song is special. The sacred staff that you see here is the tree, and its armbands are the lorikeets that climb on that tree. The arms that branch out from the tree are the Yolŋu, the children of the earth.

AC Mandawuy, you've been so generous and taught us so much today, and yet I feel we've only just begun. Perhaps a three-day conference on Yothu Yindi will be the next step. I for one, hope that we will one day see a Treaty in Australia. And I certainly hope that the Yolŋu, and the rest of us with you, will continue to sing and dance under the honey sun for a long time to come. Thank-you for being with us today.

MY Thank-you.

Baywara 'Olive Python', ancestor of the Gälpu Yolŋu (Galarrwuy Yunupiŋu 1991).

rirrakay-dhu<u>d</u>akthun

'Djäpana: Sunset Dreaming' (II/16)

'Djäpana: Sunset Dreaming' was Mandawuy's first original song. It was composed at Galiwin'ku in 1983, three years before Yothu Yindi's formation, while Mandawuy was Assistant Principal of Shepherdson College. He received guidance in its composition from his relatives in Soft Sands, which in 1982 had become the first band from Arnhem land to tour outside Australia.

In Yolŋu tradition, *djäpana* 'coral sunset' is the coral-hued haze that each day spills across the clouds and horizon with the setting sun. It is the closing subject of the Gumatj *Manikay* series that recounts the fate of fair-skinned Bayini sailors who centuries ago visited the Gumatj homeland of Bawaka. Travelling with them was a beautiful young foreign woman named Djotarra who the Bayini had captured and kept chained in the hull of their boat. When the Bayini eventually set sail from Bawaka into the glorious *djäpana* sunset, their boat struck a hidden rock drowning all aboard. Its eternal wreckage can be seen in Bawaka's coastal waters today in the form of the island Binhanhaŋay.

The island of Binhanhaŋay off Bakawa where Djotarra now lies (Aaron Corn 2005).

Gumatj *Manikay* items on the subject of *djäpana* describe the beautiful spectacle of the coral sunset, and lament the *warwu* 'sorrow' of Djotarra's unjust death alongside her Bayini captors. To this day, the Dhuwa children of Gumatj women are endearingly described as *mätjala* 'driftwood', the wood that splintered from the hull in which Djotarra was held captive.

In 'Djäpana: Sunset Dreaming', Mandawuy quotes lyrics from this *Manikay* subject to express his own sorrow for the wife and young daughters he had left behind at Yirrkala while working at Galiwin'ku. In the song's third verse, the unfairness of Djotarra's fair-skinned Bayini captors is also paralleled with the unfairness of contemporary Balanda who failed to recognise the hereditary rights of Yolŋu over their sacred homelands.

Mandawuy speaks

66 'Djäpana' is special for me. It was my first song and I wrote it one evening in 1983 while I was teaching as an Assistant Principal at Shepherdson College in Galiwin'ku. It was a Friday evening and I worked on it past midnight. Then on the morning after, I played it for the first time with Soft Sands who had just toured North America. Writing 'Djäpana' was very exciting for me and it set the pace for my future involvement with Yothu Yindi. At the time I wrote 'Djäpana', the Yolŋu side of my upbringing was starting to sink in. By then I was in my late twenties, and beginning to work out how to express myself using Gumatj *Manikay*.

You see, I was living there at Galiwin'ku on my own and I was really missing my family at Yirrkala. When *djäpana* is sung in our *Manikay*, it's an expression of sadness for the departed or whoever you're thinking about at that particular moment. That time of day, when the sun begins to set filling the clouds and the horizon with a yellow glow, it makes you think about the past, the future and the present all in one. I picked *djäpana* as a subject for this song because we see that spectacle almost every day of our lives. In a true Yolŋu sense, it gave me a way of expressing just how much I missed my family at that time. **"**

the music video

The music video for 'Djäpana' was filmed at Gunyaŋara to capture the stunning beauty of the coral sunset. Against this natural backdrop, Mandawuy leads the band and his family in two traditional dance subjects from the Gumatj series for Bawaka, *djäpana* 'coral sunset' and *mända* 'octopus'. For *djäpana*, the dancers each stretch one hand up towards the sun, and later, the band repeats this movement as they stand on rocky outcrops dotted along the coast of Gunyaŋara. In this latter scene, the musicians

Mandawuy dances *mända* with his family at Gunyaŋara, and visits the Redfern community in Sydney in 'Djäpana' (Yothu Yindi 1991).

wear sarongs patterned with a Gumatj *djäpana* design, and have painted on their fronts a sacred Gumatj design representing *mä<u>nd</u>a* as he hides among the corals beneath the sea's glassy surface. His changing colours are reflected in the coral hues seen above in clouds on the horizon at sunset. Back on the shore, *mä<u>nd</u>a* is further depicted by quartets of dancers who press their hands together in crossed pairs. Intercut with these scenes at Gunyaŋara is footage of Mandawuy visiting the Redfern Indigenous community in Sydney, and teaching Yolŋu children at Yirrkala how to paint and sing *djäpana*.

further listening

'Djäpana: Sunset Dreaming' (I/5, II/3, V/8)

These tracks feature other arrangements of this song. The first opens with the original line, 'Look at the sun sinking like a ship', which refers to the sinking Bayini vessel.

'Yirrmala "Hull"' (IV/12); 'Rräma "Coral Sunset Clouds"' (V/7)

These are two traditional *Manikay* items from the Gumatj series for Bawaka. *Yirrmala* is the hull in which Djotarra was chained. 'Rräma' is the track that precedes 'Djäpana' on *One Blood*, and it ends with the distinctive vocables, '*Ap wi*', which are immediately again heard at the opening of 'Djäpana'.

lyrics and translation

chorus *Wo djäpana* Oh coral sunset
Wo warwu Oh sorrow
Wo rramani Oh coral sunset clouds
Wo galaŋgarri Oh coral sunset

makarr 1
Ap wi, ap wi [× 2]
Djäpana wolutju Coral sunset
Dhurulama ŋunhawarrtji Fading yonder
Djäpana Coral sunset
Warwu galaŋgarri Mournful coral sunset
Rrepa ŋunhawarrtji, djäpana Falls yonder, coral sunset
Warwu goluŋnha Sadly falling
Ap wi, ap wi [× 2]

verse 1 Look at the sun falling from the sky
And the sunset takes my mind
Back to my homeland
Far away

verse 2 It's a story planted in my mind
It's so clear, I remember
Oh my, oh my
Sunset dreaming

chorus ...

verse 3 Hey, you people out there
How come you ain't fair
To the people of the land?
Try my, try my, sunset dreaming

chorus ...

makarr 2
Ap wi, ap wi [× 3]
Djäpana, warwuwu Coral sunset, sorrow
Djikulu Coral sunset
Dhuruluŋala Fading
Wolutju, warwuwu Coral sunset, sorrow

Rrepa ŋunhawarrtji, dhurulama   Darkening yonder, fading
Djäpana warwu goluŋnha   Coral sunset sadly falling
Ap wi, ap wi [× 4]

chorus ...

verse 4 Hey you children of the land
Don't be fooled by the Balanda ways
It will cause sorrow and woe
For our people and our land

chorus ...

coda   So live it up, live it up
Live it up, live it up
With sunset dreaming

'Djäpana: Sunset Dreaming'

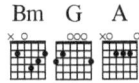

Wo_____ djä-pa-na,___   Wo_____ war-wu,

_____   Wo_____ rra-ma-ni,_____

Wo_____ ga-laŋ-ga-rri_____   Ap wi,

ap   wi,   Djä-pa-na_____   wo-lu-tju,

Dhu-ra-la-ma ŋu-nha-warr-tji,_ djä-pa-na, War - wu_____

ga-laŋ-ga-rri, Rre-pa ŋu-nha-warr-tji, djä-pa-na war - wu go-luŋ-nha

19
Bm A G A
3
Ap wi, ap wi, Ap wi, ap wi, Look at the
23
Bm A Bm
sun fall-ing from the sky, And the sun-set takes my
26
A G A
mind, Back to my home-land, Far a-
29
Bm Bm
way, It's a sto-ry (It's a sto-ry)
32
A Bm A
plant-ed in my mind, It's so clear (It's so clear), I re-mem-ber (I re-mem-ber), Oh
35
G A Bm
my (Oh my), oh my (oh my), Sun-set dream-ing (dream-ing)
38
Bm A
Wo djä-pa-na,

41
Bm
Wo___ war-wu,___ Wo___ rra-ma-ni,
44
A
Bm
3
___ Wo___ ga-laŋ-ga-rri___
47
A
(out there)
Hey (hey, you peo-ple), you peo-ple out there, How
49
Bm
come (How come) you ain't fair___ (you___ ain't fair), To the
51
A
peo-ple (to the peo-ple) of the land? (of the land?) Try
53
G
A
Bm
my (try my), try my (try my), sun-set dream-ing (dream-ing)___
56
Bm
A
___ Wo___ djä-pa-na,___

82 Bm A
Wo rra-ma-ni,
85 3 Bm 3
Wo ga-laŋ-ga-rri, Hey you
87 A
child-ren (Hey you child-ren) of the land (of the land), Don't be
89 3
fooled (Don't be fooled) by the Ba - lan - da ways
90 Bm 3
(by the Ba-lan-da ways), It will cause (It will cause)
92 A 3
sor - row and woe, For our peo-ple (For our peo - ple) and our land
94 Bm A
(and our land) Wo djä-pa-na,

97
Wo_____   war - wu,_____

99
Wo_____   rra - ma - ni,_____

101
Wo_____   ga-laŋ-ga-rri,_____   So live it up

103
___   (live it up)   Live it up___   (live it up),   live it up

105
___   (live it up),   Live it up___   (live it up), with sun- set

107
dream   -   ing

Wo_____ war - wu,_____

Wo_____ rra - ma - ni,_____

Wo_____ ga-laŋ-ga-rri,_____ So live it up

___ (live it up) Live it up___ (live it up), live it up

___ (live it up), Live it up___ (live it up), with sun- set

dream - ing

'Mainstream' (II/8)

'Mainstream' was composed in 1986 as Mandawuy completed his Bachelor of Arts in Education at Deakin University. Throughout his career and studies in education, he had always been challenged by the Balanda notion that a 'mainstream' education in English alone could fully serve the needs of a Yolŋu student. Reflecting on his own schooling under the Yirrkala Mission in his Boyer Lecture of 1993, Mandawuy recalled that 'a lot of what motivated those white teachers was the view that it was only when Yolŋu stopped being Yolŋu, that we could be Australians' (Yunupiŋu 1994: 116).

And so in 1986, when confronted with the task of writing a university assignment on the educational needs of Indigenous students, Mandawuy responded in a classically Yolŋu way. He composed 'Mainstream' as his treatise on bicultural learning and submitted it for assessment. His lecturer, Helen Verran, awarded it a High Distinction, and its inner logic became central to Yolŋu thinking about bicultural education.

To make its point, 'Mainstream' draws on two traditional models for balance between different bodies of people within Yolŋu society: *yothu-yindi* 'child-mother' and *gaṉma* 'converging currents'. The first two verses reflect the *yothu-yindi* bond between Mandawuy's Gumatj daughters and their Rirratjiŋu mother. The 'six pretty girls' of the first verse are his six daughters, and he sees their reflections in the water while he simultaneously hears the voices of Gumatj ancestors past. The monsoon clouds, thunder and spear grass cited in the second verse are sacred subjects of the girls' *ŋäṉdipulu* 'mother's group', the Rirratjiŋu *mala*.

Alternatively, the 'yellow foam' mentioned in the song's first verse is a reference to sacred *gaṉma* sites where the currents of waters owned by different Yirritja *mala* meet. Here, Mandawuy specifically refers to the relationship between the Gumatj and the Wangurri as *yapapulu* 'sister groups', as *mala* of equal social standing within Yolŋu society, and the *gaṉma* site located on the Gumatj homeland of Biranybirany. The *djikuṉguṉ* 'yellow foam'

Mandawuy Yunupiŋu, Wiṯiyana Marika and Milkayŋu Munuŋgurr in 'Mainstream' (Yothu Yindi 1989).

found there is created by the mingling of saltwater and freshwater currents, and symbolises productive interaction between two equal forces that cannot assimilate each other. This reflects in the way that different Yirritja *mala*, and different Dhuwu *mala* for that matter, can maintain their separateness while joining forces to mount ceremonies together.

In the third verse of 'Mainstream', Mandawuy then expands on these traditional models for social balance to envision an Australia in which 'black and white' live together in equality and mutual respect. However, central to this vision is the continuance of Yolŋu traditions, the only 'mainstream' to have existed within Yolŋu society for countless millennia. As Mandawuy summarises in the song's chorus, Yolŋu will continue to live 'in the mainstream' of their own traditions under the 'one dream' of the *Rom* 'Law' passed on to them from their original ancestors.

Mandawuy speaks

66 'Mainstream' is a song that was written when I was going through tertiary studies way back in 1986. It would have been around the third song that I had written. I wrote this song reflecting my family situation at that time, and also, aspects of the negotiated curriculum for two-way education that we were then developing for children attending schools in Yolŋu communities. We have our own intellectual traditions, which in our schools, we wanted to be on equal footing with Balanda knowledge. On a political level, Indigenous and non-Indigenous Australians can complement each other just like the Yolŋu and Balanda parts to our two-way school curriculum, though personally, I live 'under one dream' and that is a Yolŋu dream. 99

the music video

Filmed in 1989, 'Mainstream' was Yothu Yindi's first music video. It features Mandawuy performing with his guitar on the beach near his home, and rare footage of one of the band's early concerts for an enthusiastic local audience at Yirrkala. Still images of Indigenous designs from throughout Australia, and news footage of rallies for Indigenous rights in Australia's southern capitals are also used throughout.

further listening

'Mainstream' (I/1, V/3)

> These tracks feature other arrangements of this song. Mandawuy sings the latter as a duet with Liam Ó Maonlaí from the Hothouse Flowers. It also features the famed traditional Irish musician, Sharon Shannon, on tin whistle.

'Mätjala' "Driftwood"' (II/11)

> This song celebrates the Rirratjiŋu–Gumatj *yothu-yindi* relationship between Wiṯiyana Marika, and his *ŋapipi* 'mother's brother', Mandawuy Yunupiŋu. As discussed with 'Djäpana: Sunset Dreaming', the Dhuwa children of Gumatj women are endearingly described as *mätjala*, the wood that splintered from the hull in which Djotarra was held captive by the Bayini at Bawaka.

lyrics and translation

verse 1 Reflections in the water I see
Six pretty girls on my mind today
Yellow foam floating down the river
Voices I hear of Yolŋu heroes

chorus *Go, go, go, go*   Come ...
Living in the mainstream
Go, go, go, go
Under one dream

verse 2 Monsoon clouds rolling over the ocean
Thunder and rain raging here tonight
Hear the sound of spear grass crying
'Cross rivers and valleys on Yolŋu land

chorus ...

bridge Come on

chorus ... [× 2]

verse 3 Reflections in the water I see
Black and white living together
Sharing dreams of the red, black and gold
Living dream time now in the Yolŋu way

chorus ... [× 2]

coda We're living together, we're living together
We're learning together, we're living together
Yolŋu (Balanda), Balanda (Yolŋu), *yo, yo, yo, yo*   ... yes
Yo, yo, yo, this is Australia

'Mainstream'

Mandawuy Yunupiŋu (Mushroom)

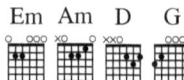

22 D Em lead guitar
Voi-ces I hear of Yol-ŋu he - roes,
25 vox G Am
Go, go, go, go, Liv-ing in the main - stream, Go, go, go,
30 D Em lead guitar
go, Un-der one dream,
33 Em Am
3
Mon-soon clouds roll-ing o-ver the o-cean,
37 D Em
Thun-der and rain rag-ing here to-night,
42 Am
Hear the sound of spear grass cry - ing, 'Cross
46 D 3 Em lead guitar
ri-vers and val-leys on Yol-ŋu land,

49
vox
G
Am
Go, go, go, go, Liv-ing in the main-stream, Go, go, go,
54
D
Em
lead guitar
go, Un-der one dream, Come on
58
Am
62
D
Em
68
Am
D
Em
73
vox
G
Am
Go, go, go, go, Liv-ing in the main-stream,
77
D
Em
to Coda
Go, go, go, go, Un-der one dream,

81

1.

2. *yidaki*   **4**

Go,   go,   go,

86   Em   Am

Re - flec - tions   in the wa-ter I see,_____

90   D   3   Em

Black and white   liv-ing to-ge - ther (we're liv-ing to-ge-

94   3

ther),   Shar-ing   dreams   of the red, black and

97   Am   D

gold   (red, black and   gold),   Liv-ing dream-time now

100   Em
lead guitar

in   the   Yol - ŋu   way,_____

102   D. S. al Coda   Coda

Go,   go,   go,   Go, go, go,

go,_____ Living in the main - stream,_   Go, go, go,

go,_____ Under one_ dream_____ We're liv-ing to-

ge-ther (we're liv-ing to-ge - ther), We're liv-ing to-ge-ther (we're liv-ing to-ge-

ther), We're learn-ing to - ge-ther (we're learn-ing to - ge -

ther), We're liv-ing to-ge - ther (we're liv-ing to-ge - ther),

Yol-ŋu (Ba-lan-da), Ba-lan-da (Yol-ŋu), yo (yo), yo

(yo), yo, This is Aus-tra-lia
(yo)

'Treaty' (II/2)

For many Australians, 1988 marked the bicentenary of a nation's birth, the 200th year since the First Fleet landed at Sydney Cove to found the British Colony of New South Wales. But for Indigenous Australians, 1988 stood for something else entirely. It marked two centuries since British colonists had declared their continent to be *terra nullius*, bereft of all previous occupation, and in doing so, denied the Indigenous peoples of Australia their humanity and their rights to homelands that were clearly theirs.

Even the Yolŋu, who knew little of their absorption into the Australian nation before the early 1930s, were stung by the presumption of *terra nullius*. Their courageous Supreme Court case against the NABALCO bauxite mine had failed in 1971, when Justice Blackburn ruled that any Yolŋu sovereignty that might ever have existed was extinguished when the First Fleet landed at Sydney Cove in 1788, and claimed Australia in the name of the British Crown (Supreme Court of Northern Territory 1971). That this singular event took place some 2700 kilometres from the nearest Yolŋu homeland and 135 years before the establishment of the first Yolŋu mission was clearly no obstacle under Australian law.

And so in 1988, amid a heady year of public events to celebrate Australia's maturity as a nation, Galarrwuy Yunupiŋu set out to complete the work that his father had started in 1962 with the Yirrkala leaders' campaign against the bauxite mine. Acting in his capacity as the elected Chair of the Northern Land Council, he collaborated with Wenten Rubuntja, his counterpart at the Central Land Council, to prepare a document that would call on the Australian government to enter into a Treaty with Indigenous Australians in recognition of their rights and freedom as Australia's original owners. Later dubbed the Barunga Statement, it took the form of a typescript bordered by sacred designs. On the left, were Yolŋu designs for four Yirritja homelands. They were balanced on the right by a Two Women Dreaming design common to central Australia and related to Dhuwa ancestors of the Yolŋu.

The Barunga Statement, 1988. Courtesy of the Australian Parliament House Art Collection.

On 12 June that year, the Barunga Statement was presented to Prime Minister Robert Hawke at the Barunga Sport and Cultural Festival under the most sacred of ceremonial conditions. His initial response was overwhelmingly positive and he promised to start negotiations towards a Treaty with Indigenous Australians within the lifetime of his parliament. But by 1990, no progress had been made and the issue had all but faded from public memory. It was then that Yothu Yindi collaborated with Peter Garrett and Paul Kelly to remind everyone of Hawke's well-publicised promise at Barunga. And together, they composed 'Treaty', which endures as Yothu Yindi's best-remembered song. 'Treaty' was remixed in

Melbourne by Filthy Lucre and rapidly gained popularity. It became the first song with lyrics in an original Australian language to top the Australian charts. Quite unexpectedly, it also charted overseas and won a string of prominent awards (see 'chronology').

The song's melody comes through its quotation of an historic *Djatpaŋarri* item composed by Rrikin Burarrwaŋa and recorded by Richard Waterman at Yirrkala in the early 1950s. With its youthful calls of encouragement to anyone dancing, the exuberance of the *Djatpaŋarri* style sets the mood and tempo for the entire song, and captures Mandawuy's nostalgia for his childhood on the Gove Peninsula before the advent of mining in 1968.

Nonetheless, the ideological heart of 'Treaty' lies in the second verse with its bold affirmation that the Yolŋu have never ceded or sold their homelands to the Crown, and that Yolŋu sovereignty was never affected by the British landing at Sydney Cove in 1788. This second verse also employs the *ganma* 'converging currents' model for social equity first used by Mandawuy in 'Mainstream'. Here, he describes Indigenous and non-Indigenous Australians as two rivers running their separate courses, and dreams of a brighter day when a Treaty will make those waters one.

Mandawuy speaks

❝ This song was written after Bob Hawke, in his famous response to the Barunga Statement of 1988, said that there would be a Treaty between Indigenous Australians and the Australian government by 1990. The intention of this song was to raise public awareness about this, so that the government would be encouraged to hold to his promise. The song became a number one hit, the first ever to be sung in a Yolŋu language, and it caught the public's imagination. Though it borrows from rock'n'roll, the whole structure of 'Treaty' is driven by the beat of the *Djatpaŋarri* that I worked into it. It was an old recording of this *Djatpaŋarri* that triggered the song. The man who originally created it passed

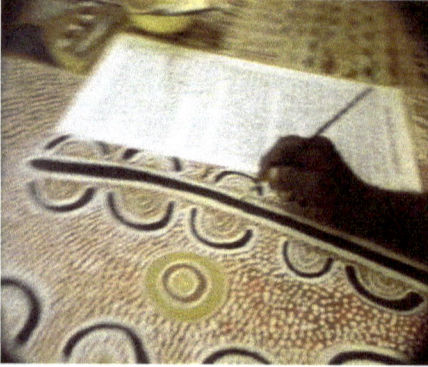

The Barunga Statement nears completion; Hawke attends the 1988 Barunga Festival; and Mandaway sings over a sacred Gumatj fire in 'Treaty' (Yothu Yindi 1991).

away a long time ago in 1978. He was a real master of the *Djaṯpaŋarri* style.**99**

the music video

There are two music videos for 'Treaty'. The first shows footage from the 1988 Barunga Festival, which includes the completion of the Barunga Statement and Prime Minister Hawke's participation there. This footage is interlaced with clips of Yothu Yindi in concert and mining operations near Yirrkala. There are also clips of Wiṯiyana leading *Djatpaŋarri* dances in the bush, and Yolŋu children playfully dancing on the beach in the spirit of the *Djatpaŋarri* style.

The second music video for 'Treaty' accompanies the Filthy Lucre remix. It shows Wiṯiyana and Milkayŋu dancing on the beach, and Mandawuy singing over a sacred Gumatj *gurtha* 'fire' with his face painted in ceremonial white. 'Treaty' blares from a boombox as Mandawuy carries it down to the beach. He hands the boombox over to the children dancing there, and passes on the song's cause to the next generation.

further listening

'Treaty' (II/16); 'Treaty '98' (V/19)

These tracks feature other arrangements of this song.

'Gapu "Water"' (II/1, III/16); 'Beyarrmak "Comic"' (II/14); 'Djaṯpa' (IV/6); 'Cora [an old supply barge]' (IV/14)

These tracks feature four historic *Djatpaŋarri* items. The third, 'Djaṯpa', is arranged with a rock accompaniment.

'Ḻuku-Wäŋawuy Manikay "Sovereignty Song" 1788' (I/15)

Composed by Galarrwuy in 1988, this song parodies the myth of *terra nullius* and traces the roots of Yolŋu sovereignty back to the original ancestors who shaped, named and populated the Yolŋu homelands of northeast Arnhem Land.

'My Kind of Life' (II/4); 'Maralitja "Saltwater Crocodile Man"' (II/5); 'Hope' (II/12); 'World of Innocence' (III/2); 'Freedom' (III/3); 'Baywara' (III/4); 'Gunitjpirr Man' (III/11); 'Our Generation'

(III/14); 'Stop That' (IV/9); 'Belief in the Future' (V/15); 'Lonely Tree' (VI/11); 'Gone Is the Land' (VI/12)

These songs respond to the NABALCO bauxite mine and recount the Yolŋu struggle to prevent it. As discussed in the previous chapter, 'Baywara' and 'Gunitjpirr Man' were composed in 1993 to mark the passing of Witiyana's father, Dadayŋu Marika, who stood as a prominent leader of this cause.

lyrics and translation

verse 1   Well I heard it on the radio
And I saw it on the television
Back in 1988
All those talking politicians
Words are easy, words are cheap
Much cheaper than our priceless land
But promises can disappear
Just like writing in the sand

chorus   Treaty yeah, Treaty now, Treaty yeah, Treaty now

makarr 1

Nhima djatpaŋarri	You dance *Djatpaŋarri*
Nhima, wälaŋ-wälaŋ	You, that's better
Nhe djatpa-yatpa	You keep dancing
Nhima gaya', nhe marrtjini	You improvise, you go on
Yakarray!	Wow!
Nhe djatpa	You dance *Djatpaŋarri*
Nhe wälaŋ	That's good
Gumurr-djararrk Gutjuk!	My poor brother!

verse 2   This land was never given up
This land was never bought and sold
The planting of the Union Jack
Never changed our law at all
Now two rivers run their course
Separated for so long

I'm dreaming of a brighter day
When the waters will be one

chorus   ...

makarr 2

Nhima gayakaya	You improvise
Nhe gaya' nhe	You improvise
Nhe gaya', nhe marrtjini	You improvise, you go on
Wälaŋ-wälaŋ	That's better
Nhe, yä!	You, ah!
Nhima djatpa	You dance *djatpaŋarri*
Nhe wälaŋ	That's good
Gumurr-djararrk yawirriny'!	My poor young men!

makarr 3

Nhe gaya', nhe marrtjini	You improvise, you improvise
Gaya' nhe, marrtjini	Go on you, go on
Gayakaya	Improvise
Nhe gaya', nhe marrtjini,	You improvise, you go on
Wälaŋ-wälaŋ	That's better
Nhima djatpa	You dance *Djatpaŋarri*
Nhe wälaŋ	That's good
Nhe gumurr-djararrk nhe, yä!	You poor things you, ah!

bridge   *i e, i e, i e e e e*
Promises disappear
Priceless land, destiny

chorus   ...

verse 1a Well I heard it on the radio
And I saw it on the television
But promises can disappear
Just like writing in the sand

chorus   ... [× 2]

coda   Come on, Treaty *ma'*, Treaty *ma'* ... now
Treaty *ma'*, Treaty *ma'*
Come on, Treaty *ma'!*

'Treaty'

Mandawuy Yunupiŋu, Galarrwuy Yunupiŋu, Milkayŋu
Munuŋgurr, Witiyana Marika, Stu Kellaway, Cal Williams, Peter
Garrett (Mushroom) and Paul Kelly (Universal)

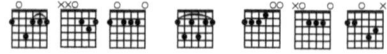

But pro-mi-ses_ can dis-ap-pear   just like wri-

ting in the   sand   Trea-ty yeah,

Trea-ty now,   Trea-ty yeah,   Trea-ty now,   *Nhi-ma*

djat-pa-ŋa-rri___   nhi-ma, wä-laŋ-wä-laŋ,   Nhe

djat-pa-yat-pa, nhi-ma ga-ya, nhe marr-tji-ni,   ya-ka-rray,___

—   Nhe djat-pa, nhe wä-laŋ,   Gu-murr-dja-rarrk Gu-

tjuk!   This land was ne-ver gi-ven_ up,

this land was ne-ver bought and sold,

The plant-ing of the U - nion Jack   ne-ver chang-

ed our law at all,   Now two ri-vers run their course

se - pa - ra - ted for so long,

I'm dream-ing of a brigh-ter day   when the

wa-ters will be one   Trea - ty yeah,

Trea - ty now,   Trea - ty yeah,   Trea - ty now,

53
F♯m
Bm/F♯ (oh)
F♯m7
Trea - ty yeah, Trea - ty now, Trea - ty yeah,
56
Bm/F♯ (oh)
NC
Trea - ty now, Nhi-ma ga-ya-ka-ya,_ nhe ga-ya' nhe, Nhe
58
ga-ya', nhe marr-tji-ni, wä-laŋ-wä-laŋ_ nhe yä,
60
3
3
Nhi-ma djaṯ - pa, nhe wä - laŋ,
62
3
Gu - murr-dja-rarrk___ ya - wi- rriny'!_ Nhe
65
ga - ya', nhe marr-tji - ni ga - ya', nhe marr-tji - ni,
66
Ga-ya-ka-ya,_ nhe ga-ya', nhe marr-tji-ni, wä-laŋ-wä-laŋ,

68
Nhi-ma djaṯ - pa, nhe wä - laŋ, Nhe
70
gu - murr-dja-rrak nhe yä! i e, i e, i
74
A
e e e e Pro-mi-ses dis-ap-pear,
78
A
F♯m
lead guitar
yiḏaki
price-less land, des-ti-ny
85
F♯m
Bm/F♯ (oh)
F♯m7
Trea - ty yeah, Trea - ty now, Trea - ty yeah,
88
Bm/F♯ (oh)
F♯m
Trea - ty now, Well I heard it on the ra - di - o
90
and I saw it on the te - le - vi - sion,

93 D

But pro - mi - ses__ can dis - ap - pear   just like wri-

95 F#m

- ting in the sand   Trea - ty yeah,

98 Bm/F# (oh)   F#m7   Bm/F# (oh)

Trea - ty now,   Trea - ty yeah,   Trea - ty now,

101 F#m   Bm/F# (oh)   F#m7

Trea - ty yeah,   Trea - ty now,   Trea - ty yeah,

104 Bm/F# (oh)   D

Trea - ty now, Come on,   Trea - ty ma',   Trea - ty ma',

107   F#m
          ⌐ 3 ⌐

Trea - ty ma',   Trea - ty ma', Come on, Trea - ty ma'!

'Tribal Voice' (III/7)

'Tribal Voice' recognises the world's many faiths, and the deep ancestral roots that all humans share. It celebrates the continuing centrality of traditional belief to life on the Gove Peninsula, despite the introduction of Christianity to Yirrkala in 1934. In the chorus, Mandawuy cries out for the survival of the Yolŋu way of life, and calls on his people to never forget the sacred *Rom* 'Law' bestowed on them by their original ancestors. As the song's end nears, Mandawuy calls on different *mala* of the Gove Peninsula to uphold this sacred covenant. He calls their names in an alternating Yirritja-Dhuwa order to evoke the *yothu-yindi* balance that sustains Yolŋu society: Gumatj and Rirratjiŋu, Wangurri and Djapu', Dhaḻwaŋu and Ḏäṯiwuy, and Maŋgalili and Gälpu.

Mandawuy speaks

❝ One Christmas at Yirrkala, I was really upset at the way that evangelists were trying to discourage us from following our culture. I wanted to send a clear message to these people about the sacredness of our Yolŋu ancestry, so 'Tribal Voice' was my response to them. There are billions of people on this Earth who have many different beliefs, and I don't believe that anyone should have to abandon their faith for another's.❞

the music video

The music video for 'Tribal Voice' opens with Yolŋu hunters stalking through the bush. Their bodies are monochrome against the bright orange of their sacred feathered adornments and the vivid green of surrounding sand palms, and they dance traditional *Buŋgul* as Mandawuy sings the opening verses. Starting with archival footage from the Tiwi Islands, there is then a lengthy sequence of clips showing traditional dances from all over the world, and candid images of Yothu Yindi touring cities in Europe and North America.

Mandawuy dances *Gäpirri* with his sacred Gumatj *bathi*; Galarrwuy sings *Manikay* over the initiates; and Yomunu and Dhaṉayil Yunupiṉu stand ready for initiation with Djaṇa Yunupiṉu in 'Tribal Voice' (Yothu Yindi 1991).

Action shifts back to Guynaṇara, where three boys are being prepared for initiation into greater knowledge of their ancestral inheritance. Mandawuy dances the Gumatj subject *Gäpirri* 'Stingray' with piercing eyes and a sacred Gumatj *bathi* 'basket' held in his mouth. This kind of *gakal* 'soloist' dance invokes the fierce power of the original ancestors, while painted and feathered baskets that accompany them are the most sacred icons of ancestral authority that can be revealed by Yolŋu elders to a public gathering. They symbolise the specific *ḻikan* 'branch' of ancestry held by each *mala*, and their use is reserved for important ceremonial acts. Galarrwuy sings *Manikay* over the boys, and his *biḻma* are painted with the Gumatj diamonds of *Bäru* 'Saltwater Crocodile'. He then paints the boys with sacred *ḻikan* designs. As the video ends, the boys stand ready for initiation beside the Gumatj elder Djaŋa Yunupiŋu, fully painted and dressed in sacred feathered cords.

further listening

'Tribal Voice' (v/10)

This track features a later arrangement of this song.

'Gäpirri "Stingray"' (ii/13)

In this song, Mandawuy describes the continuing ancestral agency of his late Gälpu and Gumatj parents. His mother is imbued with the Gälpu ancestor, Baywara 'Olive Python',

lyrics and translation

verse 1

> There's a wakening of a rainbow dawn
> And the sun will rise up high
> There's a whisper in the morning light
> Saying 'Get up and meet the day'

verse 2

> Well inside my mind there's a tribal voice
> And it's speaking to me ev'ryday
> And all I have to do is to make a choice
> 'Cause I know there is no other way

chorus 1

> All the people
> In the world are dreaming (get up, stand up)
> Some of us cry, cry, cry
> For the rights of survival now (get up, stand up)
> Saying 'Come on, come on
> Stand up for your rights' (get up, stand up)
> While others don't give a damn
> They're all waiting for a perfect day
> You'd better get up and fight for your rights
> Don't be afraid of the move you make
> You'd better listen to your tribal voice
> Pick him up, Gutjuk [Gurrumul]

chorus 2

> All the people
> In the world are dreaming (get up, stand up)
> Some of us cry, cry, cry
> For the rights of survival now (get up, stand up)
> Saying 'Come on, come on,
> Stand up for your rights' (get up, stand up)
> While others don't give a damn
> They're all waiting for a perfect day
> You'd better get up and fight for your rights
> Don't be afraid of the move you make
> You'd better listen to your tribal voice
> You'd better listen to your tribal voice

bridge

> *Yaka menguŋa nhuŋuway Rom*   Don't forget your Law
> *Dhuwala buŋgul gakal ga ḻikan*   This sacred dance and branch
> *Burrulaŋ* [Wiṯiyana], *biḻma ga yiḏaki*

verse 3

> Well I wonder if it's part of history
> Full of influence and mystery
> Come now the spirits of my people who have just gone before
> Into the future of another day

chorus 2   ...

coda   You'd better listen to your tribal voice
    You'd better listen to your tribal voice
    (You'd better listen to your) Gumatj (voice)
    (You'd better listen to your) Rirratjiŋu (voice)
    (You'd better listen to your) Wangurri (voice)
    (You'd better listen to your) Djapu' (voice)
    (You'd better listen to your) Dhaḻwaŋu (voice)
    (You'd better listen to your) Ḏäṯiwuy (voice)
    (You'd better listen to your) Maŋgalili (voice)
    (You'd better listen to your) Gälpu (voice)
    You'd better listen to your tribal voice (get up, stand up)!

'Tribal Voice'

Mandawuy Yunupiŋu (Mushroom)

There's a wake-ning of a rain-bow dawn and the sun will rise up high,___ There's a whis-per in the morn-ing light say-ing 'Get up and meet the day'___ Well in-side my mind there's a tri - bal voice and it's speak-ing to me e - v'ry-day,____   And

all I have to do is   to   make a   choice   'cause I

know there is no o - ther way,_____   All the peo-ple____

____ in the world are dream - ing__   (get up, stand up), Some of us

cry, cry, cry_____   for the rights of sur - vi - val now

(get up, stand up), Say - ing   'come on,   come on,____

stand up   for your rights'____   (get up, stand up),   While

37 Bm   Em

o - thers____ don't give a damn,   they're all

39 Bm   Em

wait-ing for a per - fect day,____   You'd bet - ter

41 Bm/D   Em

get up and fight for your rights,____   don't be a -

43 Bm/D   Em

fraid of the move you make,__   You'd bet - ter

45 Bm/D   Em

lis - ten to your tri - bal   voice,____   Pick him up, Gu - tjuk

47 *lead guitar*

50

All the   peo - ple____

____ in the world are   dream - ing__   (get up, stand up), Some of us

cry, cry, cry____   for the rights of   sur - vi - val   now,____

(get up,   stand up),   Say - ing   'come on,   come   on,____

stand up   for   your   rights'____   (get up, stand up),   While

o - thers____   don't   give   a   damn,   they're all

71
Bm   Em

wait - ing for a   per - fect day,___   You'd bet - ter

73
Bm   Em

get up and fight for your rights,___   don't be a -

75
Bm/D   Em

fraid of the move you make,___   You'd bet - ter

77
Bm/D   Em

lis - ten to your tri - bal voice,___   You'd bet - ter

79
Bm/D   Em   *yidaki*

lis - ten to your tri - bal voice___

82
                                    6

spoken *Ya-ka men-gu-ŋa nhu-ŋu-way Rom, dhu-wa-la buŋ-gul ga-kal li-kan.*
          Bu-rru-laŋ, bil-ma ga yi-da-ki!

88   *lead guitar*   Bm
       7   **3**

                    Well I won-der if it's part of his-

- to - ry,   full of in - flu - ence and mys - te - ry,_

— Come now the spi - rits of my peo- ple who have

just gone be - fore in - to the fu - ture of a - no - ther day,

All the peo-ple_____ in the world are

dream - ing_ (get up, stand up), Some of us cry, cry, cry_____

for the rights of sur - vi - val now_ (get up, stand up), Say-ing

'come on, come on,_____ stand up for your rights'_____

118
Bm   Em

(get up, stand up), While o - thers__ don't give a damn,   they're all

121 Bm   Em

wai -ting for a   per - fect   day,___   You'd bet - ter

123 Bm   Em

get up and fight for your rights,___   Don't be a -

125 Bm/D   x 4 Em

fraid   of   the move you   make,____   You'd bet - ter

127 Bm/D   Em

lis - ten to your tri - bal   voice,____   (You'd bet - ter

129 Bm/D   Em

lis - ten to   your tri - bal   voice,____   You'd bet - ter
Gu-matj

131 Bm/D   Em

lis - ten to your tri - bal   voice,____   You'd bet - ter
Ri- rra-tji-ŋu__

133 Bm/D   Em

lis - ten to your tri - bal   voice,___   You'd bet - ter
           Wan-gu-rri

135 Bm/D   Em

lis - ten to your tri - bal   voice,___   You'd bet - ter
           Dja-pu'___

137 Bm/D   Em

lis - ten to your tri - bal   voice (get up,   stand up), You'd bet - ter
           Dhal̲-wa-ŋu

139 Bm/D   Em

lis - ten to your tri - bal   voice (get up, stand up), You'd bet - ter
           Dä-t̲i - wuy

141 Bm/D   Em

lis - ten to your tri - bal___   voice (get up, stand up), You'd bet - ter
           Maŋ-ga-li - li___

143 Bm/D   Em

lis - ten to your tri - bal___ voice (get up, stand up), You'd bet - ter
           Gäl - pu___

145 Bm/D   Em   **4**

lis - ten to your tri - bal voice (get up, stand up)!

'Timeless Land' (III/1)

Some eighty-five kilometres west of central Sydney, in the town of Katoomba in the Blue Mountains, there is a gargantuan site that is sacred to the local Gundungurra people. Known in English as the Three Sisters, these three rocky peaks are traditionally associated with a constellation overhead that twinkles almost invisibly against the Milky Way. The ancient Greeks named this constellation the Pleiades 'Seven Sisters', which parallels its far older name in Yolŋu-Matha, *Djulpan* 'Seven Sisters'.

When Yothu Yindi stayed in Katoomba following the release of *Tribal Voice*, Mandawuy and Wiṯiyana felt an immediate response to the Three Sisters. It reminded them of the towering sand dunes on the Gumatj homeland of Dhanaya that the Yolŋu associate with *Djulpan*, and of the rocky escarpment on the Rirratjiŋu homeland of Yalaŋbara where hunters stalk agile wallabies. They could feel the Three Sisters calling on them to sing of their timeless beauty, and to remember all the traditional owners whose souls had departed there for their ancestral realm beyond. The song that resulted was 'Timeless Land'.

Manikay is sung by Wiṯiyana four times in 'Timeless Land'. His first two passages directly quote the Rirratjiŋu subject *muḻpiya'* 'wallaby', which describes how hunters stalk this prey through the rocky escarpment country of Yalaŋbara. It also describes how *muḻpiya'* surround themselves with leafy stringy-bark shelters for protection when resting, and how the Rirratjiŋu recreate these structures when performing purification ceremonies. When the weary *muḻpiya'* sense the presence of hunters, they quickly take flight.

'Timeless Land' concludes with two bare *Manikay* items from the series for the Gumatj homeland of Guḻkuḻa. Their subject is *mambuḻmambuḻ* 'red kangaroo meat', which describes how the Gumatj share the spoils of the hunt with all of their kin, whether Dhuwa or Yirritja. Again, this juxtaposition of Rirratjiŋu and Gumatj *Manikay* subjects reflects the *yothu-yindi* relationship between these two *mala*. And in a subtle twist that attests to

Above: The Three Sisters at Katoomba (Aaron Corn 2004).
Below: *Djulpan*. Courtesy of NASA.

Mandawuy sings under the Milky Way; Wiṯiyana Marika, Malati Yunupiŋu, Makuma Yunupiŋu and Maŋatjay Yunupiŋu perform *mambulmambul* in 'Timeless Land' (Yothu Yindi 1993).

Wiṯiyana's true mastery of the *Manikay* tradition, he sings *mambulmambul* in his own Rirratjiŋu tongue to demonstrate that he is the child of a Gumatj mother.

Mandawuy speaks

❝ 'Timeless Land' was composed after our visit to the famous Blue Mountains and the place there that traditional owners identify as the Three Sisters. The song refers to these Great Sisters and links their ancestral identity to the way that we Yolŋu relate to land through our traditional *Manikay*. We mixed those two elements together and came up with 'Timeless Land'. Basically, it's a song that reflects our own Yolŋu ties to land and how there are fundamental ways of understanding the land in Australia that can be appreciated across different cultures. It describes our way of seeing the land, and of appreciating the Indigenous peoples who have expressed the land for countless generations. 99

the music video

The music video for 'Timeless Land' uses time-lapse photography to capture the ancient beauty of the Australian landscape. Scenes filmed in South Australia's Coorong National Park show Mandawuy singing on a beach underneath the Milky Way, and clay-encrusted dancers moving across mud plains like the original ancestors as Wiṯiyana sings *Manikay*.

further listening

'Dhum'thum "Wallaby"' (II/6)

This track features a traditional Rirratjiŋu *Manikay* item on the subject of *muḻpiya'* 'wallaby'. *Muḻpiya'* and *dhum'thum* are synonyms.

'Gamaḏaḻa [red kangaroo escarpment]' (I/6); 'Garrtjambal "Red Kangaroo"' (I/7); 'Mambuḻmambuḻ "Red Kangaroo Meat"' (I/8)

These tracks feature three traditional items from the Gumatj *Manikay* series for Guḻkuḻa.

'One Blood' (v/2)

Mandawuy composed this song to mark the 2000 Olympic Games in Sydney. It quotes the *laykarrambu* subject from the Gumatj *Manikay* series for the Guḻkuḻa. Here *laykarrambu* symbolises the prowess of Olympic athletes, and his blood represents the shared ancestry of all humanity.

'Our Land' (v/17)

Instead of *muḻpiya'* and *mambuḻmambuḻ*, this new setting of 'Timeless Land' quotes the *Manikay* subject of *nyiŋanyiŋa* 'anchovy' from the Gumatj series for Dhanaya. These shiny little fish dart about in the water at lightning speed, just as *Djulpan* shimmers almost invisibly in the night sky. This shimmering effect is called *diṯimurru*, which was the name given to Yothu Yindi's compilation of early music videos.

'Gunumarra "Anchovy"' (I/13, I/14); 'Nyiŋanyiŋa "Anchovy"' (V/16)

lyrics and translation

verse 1   I feel the spirits of the great sisters
Calling on me to sing
This is the learning of the great story
I'll tell you about this place
From the edge of the mountains, fly down the valley
Down where the Snowy River flows
Follow the water down to the ocean
Bring back the memory

chorus   This is the timeless land
This is our land
This is the timeless land
This is our land

makarr A1

Ŋayi nyin buma	Preparing it
Lalarryuman	The leafy shelter
Ŋayi nyin buma	Preparing it
Gundimulkyuman	The leafy shelter
Wangarrṯja	At Wangarr
Ŋurrmiŋurrmi	The leafy ground sculpture
Raywuyun	Looking askance
Buma, raywuyun	Preparing, looking askance
Ŋarrku djuṯutjtuṯu	Hunted everywhere
Ŋarrku, nawanawa	Hunted, aware
Biŋga, biŋga	Be wary, be wary
Biŋga, biŋga	Be wary, be wary
Butjurrbutjurr	Hopping

Raywu raywu	Looking askance
Ŋarrku djuṯutjtuṯu	Hunted everywhere
Gundimulkyuman	The leafy shelter

verse 2   Just like the wise man taught me the beauty
Of the creation times
The point where the mountain meets with the sky
Sparks a fire within my soul
Watching mother nature around me
Women Creators' history
Finding old people up in these mountains
Sharing the same old song

chorus   ... [× 2]

makarr A2

Ŋarrku djuṯutjtuṯu	Hunted everywhere
Ŋarrku djuṯutjtuṯu	Hunted everywhere
Ŋarrku, nawanawa	Hunted, aware
Mulu rarrirarri	Lying in the leafy ground hollow
Ŋayi nyin buma	Preparing it
Djilpiṉli, lalarrkumbi	Rocky escarpment, the leafy shelter
Biŋga, biŋga	Be wary, be wary
Biŋga, biŋga	Be wary, be wary
Butjurrbutjurr	Hopping
Raywu raywu	Looking askance
Ŋayi nyin buma	Preparing it
Djilpiṉli	Rocky escarpment
Djarrambal buma	Preparing the stringybark leaves
Molk niny buma	Preparing the ground sculpture
Wangarrtja	At Wangarr
Wangarrminy	At Wangarr
Ŋarrku djuṯutjtuṯu	Hunted everywhere
(The ocean, the valleys, the mountains, the sisters)	

chorus   ... [× 2]

makarr B1

Galala	Eating
Galala	Eating
Dhulmudhulmu	Eating
Mambuḻmambuḻ	Red kangaroo

Ŋurruwu mambirri	Lurking behind the red grevillea
Ŋurruwu nyenyirri	Lurking behind the red grevillea
Raypinybiny	Rare meat
Raypinybiny	Rare meat
Garrayal gulkthuwan	Rare meat torn
Garrayal nokan	Its fat eaten
Gamaḏuḏu	Fatty rare meat
Gamaḏuḏu	Fatty rare meat
Yolthu nokan?	Who is eating?
Wultjaŋgirryu	All Dhuwa people
Galala	Eating
Galala	Eating
Yolthu nokan?	Who is eating?
Maralitja Barrupayu	Yirritja Saltwater Crocodile people
Rarrkararrka	Yirritja Saltwater Crocodile people
Rarrkararrka	Yirritja Saltwater Crocodile people
Ŋunybuŋunybu	Yirritja Saltwater Crocodile people
Dharpayarra, galala	Yirritja Ironwood people, eating

makarr B2

Galala	Eating
Galala	Eating
Dhukululu	Yirritja Saltwater Crocodile people
Ŋunybuŋunybu	Yirritja Saltwater Crocodile people
Barrupa Rarrkararrka	Yirritja Saltwater Crocodile people
Muniwayŋuru	Yirritja Saltwater Crocodile people
Melŋamthunmi	Baiting
Melŋamthunmi	Baiting
Galala	Eating
Dhulmudhulmu	Eating
Mambulmambul	Red kangaroo
Dhulmudhulmu	Eating
Nokan, ŋarruŋ	Eating, eating
Nokan, ŋarruŋ	Eating, eating
Djatja nokan	Red kangaroo eaten
Raypinybiny [× 2]	Rare meat [× 2]
Gamaḏuḏu, galala,	Fatty rare meat, eating
Dhulmudhulmu mambul	Eating red kangaroo

'Timeless Land'

Mandawuy Yunupiŋu, Witiyana Marika, Stu Kellaway and David Bridie (Mushroom)

I feel the spi-rits of the great sis-ters call-ing on me to sing,

This is the learn-ing_ of the great sto-ry, I'll tell you a-bout this place,

From the edge of the moun-tains, fly down the val-ley,_

down where the Sno - wy Ri - ver flows,

Fol - low the wa - ter___ down to the o - cean,

bring back the mem - o - ry

This is the time - less land,___

This is our land   *Ḏa-yi nyin bu - ma, la - larr-yu-*

man,   Ḏa-yi nyin bu - ma, gun-di - mulk-yu - man___

Wan-garr-tja___ ŋurr-mi-ŋurr - mi,   Ray-wu-yun, bu -

38

ma, ray - wu - yun,   Ḍarr-ku dju - ṯu - tju - ṯu,___

40   F   Gm

__ ŋarr-ku__ na-wa-na-wa, Biŋ-ga, biŋ-ga,___   biŋ-ga,___

43 Dm   F   Gm

biŋ - ga,__   Bu-tjurr-bu-tjurr   ray-wu   ray-wu,

47 Dm

Ḍarr-ku dju - ṯu - tju - ṯu___   gun- di- mulk -yu-

49 F   Gm

Just   like   the wise   man who taught me   the beau - ty
man

51 Dm   F

of the cre-a-tion times,   The point where the moun-tain

54 Gm   Dm

meets with the sky sparks a fi - re with-in my soul,

57   F   Gm

Watch-ing   mo - ther___   na - ture   a - round   me,___

59   Dm   F

Wo - men Cre-a -tors' his - to - ry,   Find-ing old peo-ple___

62   Gm   Dm

up in   these moun-tains, sha - ring the same old song

65   Am   F   Dm
x 4

This is   the time - less land,_____   This is   our   land

68   NC

Darr-ku___   dju - tu - tju - tu,_____   ŋarr - ku___

71

dju - tu - tju - tu,___   Darr-ku, na - wa   -   na - wa,_____

73

mu - lu___   ra - rri - ra - rri,___

Ḍa-yi ɲin bu - ma, Djil - piṉ - li,   la - larr- kum-bi,

Biŋ- ga,   biŋ - ga,_____   biŋ - ga,_____   biŋ - ga,__

Bu- tjurr - bu - tjurr,   ray-wu__   ray-wu, __

Ḍa-yi ɲin bu - ma, Djil - piṉ - li,   Dja-rram- bal, bu - ma

molk niny bu-ma,_   Wan-garr-tja, Wan - garr- miny,___   Ḍarr- ku__

dju- ṯu- tju-ṯu,_   (The o - cean,   the val - leys,   the moun- tains,

the sis - ters)   This is the time-less land,_____

95
Dm
NC
This is our_ land
Ga-la - la_
98
ga - la - la,_
Dhul - mu - dhul - mu_
100
mam - bul̲ - mam-bul̲,_
Ŋu - rru - wu mam - bi - rri,
102
3
ŋu - rru - wu nye - nyi - rri,
Ray - piny - biny,_
104
ray - piny - biny,_
Ga-rra - yal gulk-thu - wan,
106
ga-rra - yal_ no - kan,_
Ga-ma - d̲u - d̲u,_
108
ga - ma-d̲u - d̲u,_
Yol - thu no - kan?
Wul - tjaŋ-girr-yu,_

Ga - la - la, _____ ga - la - la, _____

Yol - thu no - kan? ____ Ma - ra - li - tja Ba - rru - pa - yu,

Rarr - ka - rra - ka ____ Rarr - ka - rarr - ka,

Ḏuny - bu - ŋuny - bu, _____ Dhar - pa - ya - rra, _____

ga - la - la ____ Ga - la - la, __

ga - la - la, _____ Dhu - ku - lu - lu __ Nuny - bu - nuny - bu, _____

Ba - rru - pa Rarr - ka - rarr - ka Mu - ni - way - ŋu - ru, __

127
Mel - ŋam - thun - mi, mel - ŋam - thun - mi,
129
Ga - la - la, dhul - mu - dhul - mu,
131
Mam - bul̲ - mam - bul̲, dhul - mu - dhul - mu,
133
No - kan, ŋa - rruŋ, no - kan, ŋa - rruŋ, Dja - tja no - kan,
136
ray - piny - biny, ray - piny - biny, Ga - ma - d̲u - d̲u,
139
ga - la - la, dhul - mu - dhul - mu mam - bul̲

'World Turning' (III/7)

'World Turning' was composed as a love song. But with its release following the demise of *terra nullius* through the pivotal Mabo judgment of 1992 (Sharp 1996), it reflected the hope for Reconciliation in Australia that many then felt. *Yothu-yindi* balance is again evident in the song's second verse, which Mandawuy sings in his mother's Gälpu tongue.

Mandawuy speaks

66 'World Turning' was originally composed as a boy-meets-girl song. It describes traditional courtship, and sharing a romance that is spiritually grounded in the way that separate Yirritja and Dhuwa ancestries complement each other. This echoes the way that Yolŋu think about the earth. While the world is turning, complementary forces will attract each

Galarrwuy advocates equality between *bathi* and law books, between Yolŋu Law and Crown Law. Courtesy of the Northern Land Council.

other, whether they're Yirritja and Dhuwa, male and female. I guess that's why 'World Turning' also influenced public attitudes toward Reconciliation. 🙶

the music video

In the music video for 'World Turning' the band wears flashy costumes with sacred feathered cords. Mandawuy later sings in his mother's Gälpu tongue over a sacred Gumatj *gurtha* 'fire' to reflect their *yothu-yindi* bond.

further listening

'Mabo' (iii/8)

This song follows 'World Turning' on *Freedom* and celebrates the repeal of *terra nullius* through the historic Mabo judgement.

lyrics and translation

verse 1   I've been looking for you
          Searching for something new
          You keep my feet on the ground
          As you make my world turn around
          Keep sending me signals
          Don't let me fall by the way

chorus   And while the world is turning right
          Show me the way to your heart
          'Cause when you call my name
          It's like the world is turning right [× 3]

verse 2   *Burrkuwurrkumi*   Feathered headband
          Raywa raywa raywayuwa   Swaying shoulder to shoulder
          Wirrkul manawuny   Forbidden girl
          Gaywa gaywa gaywayuwa   Come, come, come here
          Ditjuman nyäku gayawak My ancestors' wisdom
          Räliya dhambal ŋayili   Has returned to this ground

chorus   ...

bridge   It's like the world is turning right
          Goin' to show me the way
          There is no turning back
          While it's turning right
          Well it's turning right while it's turning right [× 2]

verse 1   ...

chorus   ...

coda   It's like the world is turning right [× 5]

'World Turning'

Mandawuy Yunupiŋu and Witiyana Marika (Mushroom)

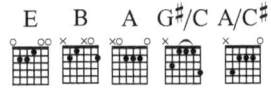

17
G♯/B♯
A/C♯
show me the way to your heart, 'Cause when you
19
A
E
to Coda
B
call my name It's like the world is
22
E
B
E
turn-ing right, It's like the world is turn-ing right
25
A
lead guitar
B
Burr-ku -
29
E
B
wurr-ku - mi ray-wa ray-wa ray-wa-yu-wa,
32
E
Wirr - kul ma - na - wuny
34
B
gay - wa gay - wa gay - wa - yu - wa,

36
E
Di - tju - man nyä - ku ga - ya - wak
38
B
rä - li - ya dham-bal ŋa - yi - li,
40
A
B
And while the world is turn-ing right,
43
G♯/B♯
A/C♯
show me the way to your heart, 'Cause when you
45
A
E
B
x 3
call my name, It's like the world is
48
E
B
E
turn-ing right, It's like the world is turn-ing right, Goin' to
51
NC
show me the way (show me the way), There is

53
no turn-ing back_____ (no turn-ing back) while it's

55
turn-ing right_____ (turn-ing right),___ Well it's

57
turn-ing right while it's turn-ing right, Well it's

59
lead guitar
turn-ing right while it's turn-ing right_____

62   D. S. al Coda   Coda   x 6   B   E
14
voice ad lib.
world is turn-ing right, It's like the

78   B   E
world   is   turn - ing   right

'Dots on the Shells' (III/13)

Composed with Neil Finn from Crowded House, Mandawuy wrote 'Dots on the Shells' in memory of his late mother. During his childhood, Mandawuy's mother would regularly take him hunting, and as they walked, they would collect spotted cowrie shells along the Gove Peninsula's beaches. Drawing on the same traditional body of Gumatj imagery as 'Djäpana', *mä<u>nd</u>a* 'octopus' hides among the corals beneath the sea's calm surface. It changes colour as the *djäpana* sunset spreads across the horizon causing bittersweet memories of Mandawuy's mother to flood back into his mind. A calm northeasterly breeze blows in from the distant horizon, also reminding Mandawuy that the wild cashews his mother used to harvest are now in season.

Mandawuy speaks

❝ I composed 'Dots on the Shells' with Neil Finn over a few days just before we recorded *Freedom*, and working on it with him was a great experience. In my younger days, I used to collect shells on the beaches between Yirrkala and Gunyaŋara with my mother. I wanted to tell everyone about her existence and how she helped me, so this song is about her, and the wisdom inscribed in the lines on her face. It's also about the places in northeast Arnhem Land where we collected shells together. The octopus mentioned in the bridge is associated with tracts of sea owned by Yirritja people. Together they are called Manbuyŋa. There are several places in Manbuyŋa between Cape Arnhem and the Wessel Islands that are associated with coral and octopus. These are owned by different Yirritja *mala*, but at each place, there's a rocky outcrop in the sea that signifies where octopus hides in the coral underneath. The changing colours of the octopus as it hides in the coral are reflected in the colours of *djäpana* as it spreads across the clouds and the horizon. ❞

Above: *Djäpana* as seen from Mandawuy's mother's mother's country, the Dhaḻwaŋu homeland of Gurrumuru (Aaron Corn 2005).

Left: Neil Finn with Mandawuy in 'Dots on the Shells' (Yothu Yindi 1993).

the music video

The music video for 'Dots on the Shells' shows Mandawuy taking his family to beaches in Darwin, where spotted cowrie shells are held up for the camera. It also contains footage of Neil Finn on stage with Yothu Yindi in Melbourne, and to accompany the song's bridge, a vibrantly coloured octopus swimming through the water.

further listening

'Dots on the Shells' (v/6)

Mandawuy sings this later arrangement of the song as a duet with Jim Kerr from Simple Minds. It also features the famed traditional Irish musician, Sharon Shannon, on accordion.

'Ŋarrpiya "Octopus"' (IV/3)

This track features a traditional Gumatj *Manikay* item on the *mända* subject.

lyrics and translation

makarr 1

Yarryarryurru gunbilk	Stretching into the horizon
Marrawulwul	The sea's calm surface
Djambi dhoru	Corals
Warrpididi	Changing colour
Dhawalinydja dhuwala	This is the season
Marrawurrtjara	Of the sea's calm surface
Dhawalinydja dhuwala	This is the season
Dhoruthuruya	Of the corals

chorus

Like the lines on your face
The answer is here
And the light in your eyes
Don't hide it away
Like the dots on the shells
They shine

makarr 2

Dhawalinydja dhuwala	This is the
Dirrmalaya	Season of the northeasterly wind
Dhawalinydja dhuwala	This is the
Luŋgurrmaya	Season of the northeasterly wind
Ya wo, ya wo	Ah oh, ah oh
ganyawuya	Wild cashew tree
Ya wo, ya wo	Ah oh, ah oh
yaŋayana	Wild cashew nuts

chorus ...

bridge

Doo-doo doo-doo doo [× 8]
Dots on shells, those dots on the shells
Come on, the water's edge goes on
Always rolling into the horizon

We'll go down where the octopus plays
Changing colour at the end of the day

chorus   ...

coda   Like the last star in the sky
Tonight
Like the lights in the city
Tonight

'Dots on the Shells'

Mandawuy Yunupiŋu and Neil Finn (Mushroom)

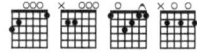

Yarr - yarr - yu - rru gun - bilk

ma - rra - wul - wul,_   Djam - bi dho - ru   warr - pi - di - di,___

Dha - wa - liny - dja   dhu - wa - la   ma - rra - wurr - tja - ra,___

Dha - wa - liny - dja dhu - wa - la   dho - ru - thu - ru - ya,___Like the lines

(the lines,___ your face)

_____ on your face,_____   The an - swer is

(your___ eyes)

here,___ And the light_____ in your eyes,

18
Don't hide it a - way, Like the dots
20
C
Bm
Em
(like the dots) on the shells, they shine
23
to Coda
Am
Dha-wa-liny-dja dhu-wa-la dirr-ma-la-ya,
26
B7
Em
Dha-wa-liny-dja dhu-wa-la luŋ-gurr-ma-ya,
28
Am
B7
Ya wo, ya wo, ga-nya-wu-ya, Ya wo, ya wo,
31
Em
D. S. al Coda
ya-ŋa-ya-na, Like the lines
Coda
F/A
(Doo
Doo-doo doo-doo doo,
33
ah,
D
Doo
doo - doo Doo-doo doo, Doo-doo doo-doo doo,

35

G⁷

ah,_____   Doo_____

Doo - doo   doo - doo   doo,   Doo - doo   doo - doo   doo,

37   G⁷

Em/B

ah,_____   Doo_____

Doo - doo   doo - doo   doo,   Doo - doo   doo - doo   doo,

39

F

ah,_____   Doo_____

Doo - doo   doo - doo   doo,   Dots on   the   shells, those

41   ah)_____   Em   Am

dots on   the shells, Come on,____   the wa - ter's edge goes on,__

44   B⁷   Em

Al - ways rol - ling in - to the ho - ri - zon,____

46   Am

We'll go down   where the   oc - to - pus__   plays,

48   B⁷   Em

Chan - ging co - lour at the end of the day,__ Like the lines

50
C
(the lines, your
D
face)
G
on your face,
The ans-wer is
53
C
(your
D
eyes)
here, And the light in your eyes,
56
G
Don't hide it a - way, Like the dots
58
C
Bm7
Em
(like the dots) on the shells, they shine,
61
C
Bm7
Like the last star in the sky, to -
64
Em
C
night, Like the lights (lights) in the ci -
67
Bm7
Em
bass guitar 6
ty, to - night

'Ghosts Spirits' (vi/6)

'Ghost Spirits' tells a tale of forbidden love that echoes the exploits of Ganbulapula, the great *mokuy* 'ghost' ancestor who hunts the stringybark forests of the Gumatj homeland, Gulkula. Ganbulapula provides valuable rules for hunting yams, honey and kangaroos, for making *yidaki*, for funeral ceremonies, and for planning marriages. A towering statue of Ganbulapula, painted with creeping yam vines, was erected at Gulkula during the first Garma Festival there in 1999. But like a wild force of nature, Ganbulapula is also unruly, unpredictable, cannibalistic and insatiably lustful. 'Ghost Spirits' opens and closes with Mandawuy singing a traditional Gumatj item from Ganbulapula's *Manikay* series for Gulkula. It describes how *ŋerrk* 'sulphur-crested cockatoo' perches on a traditional bark shelter in the twilight. His cries alert the young lovers to the danger of their romance. The lovers wonder if they have been trapped in a spell, and recoil at the thought of the damage they could do to themselves and their families.

Mandawuy speaks

66 The traditional *Manikay* in 'Ghost Spirits' is associated with Gulkula, and describes *ŋerrk* crying at sunset and into the evening twilight. This theme runs like a vein through the rest of the song as it explores a more serious side to the boy-meets-girl romance. 99

the music video

The music video for 'Ghost Spirits' is awash with Ganbulapula's imagery for Gulkula. Its scenes are bathed in the smoky haze of *wärrarra* 'blood red sunset', which Ganbulapula creates by lighting fires to flush his prey out of the forest. As Mandawuy sings *ŋerrk*, he clutches forward with a traditional Gumatj dance movement that shows how Ganbulapula collects wild *guku* 'honey' from beehives hidden up in the forest canopy.

Above: Mandawuy dances *guku* in 'Ghost Spirits' (Yothu Yindi 2000).

Left: The towering statue of Ganbulapula at Gulkula (Aaron Corn 2004). Courtesy of the Yothu Yindi Foundation.

further listening

'Ṉerrk "Sulphur-Crested Cockatoo"' (III/5); 'Ḻorrpu "Sulphur-Crested Cockatoo"' (IV/10); 'Laykarrambu "Male Red Kangaroo"' (V/1); 'Yarryurru "Red Kangaroo Spear"' (V/18)

These tracks feature four traditional items from the Gumatj *Manikay* series for Gulkula.

'Yolŋu Woman' (I/2); 'My Kind of Life' (II/4); 'Dharpa "Tree"' (II/9); 'Surfin' the Log' (VI/3); 'Bush' (VI/5); 'Wirrku<u>l</u> "Maiden" Girl' (VI/10); 'Gone Is the Land' (VI/12)

These tracks feature other original songs that incorporate sacred subjects associated with Ganbulapula.

lyrics with translation

makarr

Ganuru, milkarri	Crying, crying
<u>L</u>orrpu ŋutjawil	Sulphur-crested cockatoo cries
Ŋäthi ba<u>d</u>ikan	Crying sulphur-crested cockatoo
Djamba malakina yaluluŋala	Bark shelter in the twilight
Ŋerrk, ŋerrk	Sulphur-crested cockatoo [× 2]

verse 1

Underneath the whistling tree
Where the shore, the shore meets the sea
Dawn's light shines on you and me
This is a place I should never be
Meeting you would be a crime
Another place, another time
Feel the pull across the line
Ghost spirits on my mind, on my mind

verse 2

Does it feel like we're getting sung?
Shadows fade, we've just begun
Right skin, you have to be the one
Must be gone before the sun
At the cry of the cockatoo
Heart beats, what can I do?
Yaka mari me and you   No quarrel ...
What was one again is two, again is two

chorus

Poison love, forbidden fruit
Take my hand, it's evil's fruit
Poison love attracting you

Attracting me, attracting you
Poison love, forbidden fruit
Don't think twice, it's evil's root
Poison love attracting you
Attracting me, attracting you

bridge Would it be so bad another time?
Would it be so bad?

verse 3
Another waits, the chosen one
Broken promises, bloodlines run
Feel the pressure against the gun
This is the game that could not be won
The situation, it seems so sad
But for the love that I could have had
Frustration drives me mad, loveless life
Would it be so bad, would it be so bad?

bridge ...

makarr a

Ganuru milkarri	Crying, crying
Lorrpu ŋutjawil	Sulphur-crested cockatoo cries
Ŋäthi baḏikan	Crying sulphur-crested cockatoo
Djamba malakina yaluluŋala	Bark shelter in the twilight

chorus ...

'Ghost Spirits'

Stu Kellaway, Makuma Yunupiŋu, Mandawuy Yunupiŋu and Lamar Lowder (Mushroom)

17
this is a place I should ne-ver be,
Meet-ing you would be a crime
19
a-no-ther place, a-no-ther time,
Feel the pull a-cross the line,
21
ghost spi-rits on my mind,
on my mind
24
2
Does it feel like we're get-ting sung?
27
Sha-dows fade, we've just be-gun
Right skin, you have to be the one,
29
must be gone be-fore the sun,
At the cry of the cock-a-too,
31
heart beats, what can I do?
Ya-ka ma-ri
me and you,

what was one a-gain is two,_   a-gain is two

Poi-son love, for-bid-den fruit,   take my hand, it's e-vil's fruit,

Poi-son love, at-tract-ing you,   at-tract-ing me,_ at-tract-ing you,

Poi-son love, for-bid-den fruit, don't think twice, it's e-vil's fruit,

Poi-son love, at-tract-ing you,   at-tract-ing me,_ at-tract-ing you

(Would it be so bad_____

a - no-ther time?_____   Would it

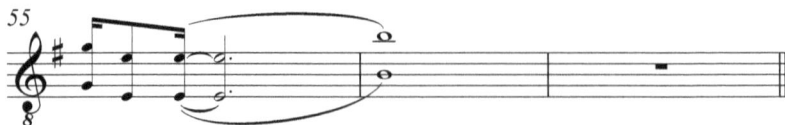

be   so   bad?)_____

A-no-ther waits, the cho-sen one,_ bro-ken pro-mi-ses, blood-lines run,

Feel the pres-sure a-gainst the gun,_ this is the game that can-not be won,

The sit-u-a-tion, it seems so sad__ but for the love that I could have had,

Frus-tra-tion drives me mad,___ love-less life, would it be so bad (Would it

be so bad),___ would it be so bad?__   (a - no-ther time?__

_____ Would it be so bad?)__ *Ga-nu-ru_*   *mil-ka- rri,_lorr-pu*

75
ŋu-tja-wil, Ŋä-thi ba-d̲i-kan,
3
78
djam-ba ma-la-ki-na ya-lu-lu-ŋa-la
80
Poi-son love, for-bid-den fruit, take my hand, it's e-vil's fruit,
82
Poi-son love, at-tract-ing you, at-tract-ing me, at-tract-ing you,
84
Poi-son love, for-bid-den fruit, don't think twice, it's e-vil's fruit,
86
Poi-son love, at-tract-ing you, at-tract-ing me, at-tract-ing you
88
playout
20

conclusion

Child and mother. The meeting of different currents. The shared ancestry of all humanity. The living wisdom of those who have gone before. The struggle for justice against insurmountable odds. And the future of another day. These are the values of equality, sharing and hope that colour Yothu Yindi's music and first brought the band to international attention. They shifted the thinking of educators in the Northern Territory, and made it legitimate for Aboriginal school children there to learn in their own languages. They captured hearts in an Australia that proudly shed the harmful conceit of *terra nullius*, and they introduced Treaty to this nation's political vocabulary. Through these achievements, they challenged many Australians like me to perceive their own country in a boldly different way.

This was Yothu Yindi's gift. A vision for a Reconciled Australia under a constitutionally enshrined Treaty, where the laws and perspectives of Indigenous peoples were not rejected and trivialised, but instead seen as integral to the Australian way of life. A Reconciled Australia where *bathi* and law books could hold equal weight. This offering has always seemed to me to be both generous and constructive. Even after the demoralising court defeat of 1971 and Hawke's unfulfilled promise of a Treaty in 1988, the Yolŋu have always held the lines of communiciation open. They continue to uphold their laws regardless, and hope that others will come to understand their plight.

While the present Northern Territory Intervention into Aboriginal child welfare brings a much needed injection of new funds into Indigenous communities, it remains unclear whether this approach truly advances Australia, or is yet another state exercise in heavy handed paternalism. For many, the Intervention's most controversial aspect is its exemption from the *Racial Discrimination Act 1975*. But most disappointing for me personally was to hear how my friends and colleagues in Arnhem Land were being so roundly ignored. Like Mandawuy, many of these

Indigenous Territorians have dedicated their lives to local initiatives in education and community development. They have worked in remote communities for decades with exceptionally limited resources. But the Intervention sent a message that they had somehow failed. It was as though we were told that all their efforts to escape poverty and build better futures for their children and grandchildren had amounted to nothing. And it was as though nothing positive had ever come of all their careful measures to ensure that local children could grow to participate in Australia's broader society, while still learning to maintain traditional relationships with kin, ancestors and country.

Mandawuy's own first steps in the 1980s to ensure that Yolŋu children would have the benefits of a bicultural education were born not out of cultural pride, but as an essential strategy for cultural survival. His parents' generation had lived through the mission era with few other competing extra-cultural influences. But with the advent of mining in 1968 and the introduction of television to Arnhem Land in the early 1980s, Yolŋu traditions now competed for young attentions with a deluge of new entertainments on screen and stereo, and all of them in English. For the first time in history, Yolŋu livelihoods within Arnhem Land were becoming impossible without English, which was required to access even the most basic of state services.

It fell upon Mandawuy's generation to ensure that the old ways were not swept away in this flood of the new. Bicultural education offered one way to ensure that local children would be grounded in their own languages and traditions before acquiring English. But the other way was even more ingenious. It was to use Yolŋu languages, and all their semantic resonances, in creative new ways that were equally entertaining. This was where Mandwuy's bold new approach to song composition came in. He took rock music and embedded within it ancestral themes and direct quotations from their Yolŋu *Manikay* tradition that his own people would instantly recognise. And in doing so, he pioneered a way for Yolŋu youth to comprehend and express the continuing relevance of their living traditions in the comtemporary world. He found a musical voice that was distinctly Australian, yet gounded within a deep tradition of Indigenous knowledge and practice that no Balanda composer could ever hope to match. It is certain that this distinctive Yothu Yindi style would never have developed if Mandawuy, Witiyana, Milkayŋu and Galarrwuy had not been gifted exponents of their own musical and ceremonial traditions, even though few outside Arnhem Land could have appreciated the sacred resonances of the band's music when it first rose to attention in the early 1990s.

Two generations of musicians in Arnhem Land have since followed in Yothu Yindi's steps. And together, they have composed thousands of original songs in their own traditional languages, which reflect the sacred identities, knowledge and values passed to them from the ancestors. The latest cohort of gifted musicians from Arnhem Land includes the Saltwater Band who also draws on the *Manikay* tradition, the Nabarlek Band who draws on the *Kunborrk* tradition of the region's west, and Yilila who draws on song traditions of the region's southeast. And most recently, the meteoric rise of Gurrumul Yunupiŋu to solo acclaim has introduced even more people around the world to the beauty and poetry of Yolŋu music.

In a world where globalisation and mass poverty forces the attrition of more and more languages and distinct regional cultures with each passing year, these exceptional achievements are to be cherished. By creating a vibrant new outlet for the use of local languages and song traditions in youthful new ways, they are now integral to the thin line that exists in regional Australia between maintenance and loss of tradition. This is indeed why Mandawuy and Witiyana, among many other Indigenous leaders nationwide, have so strongly supported the National Recording Project for Indigenous Performance in Australia. With the masters of Australia's unique Indigenous music and dance traditions now falling ill and passing away at an alarming rate, many Indigenous communities have identified an immediate need to record and archive their knowledge for future generations. Unless serious resources are soon committed to empowering Indigenous communities to achieve this ambitious goal, these opportunities will be lost forever.

Whenever I visit Parliament House in Canberra, I think of the opportunities we have already missed. I walk through the public galleries where the 1963 Yirrkala Petition, the 1968 Wuyal Petition and the 1988 Barunga Statement rest in silence, and I marvel at the weeks it must have taken to apply such delicate lines to each bark panel. I try to imagine how disheartened Yolŋu communities must have felt as each subsequent bid for recognition resulted in disappointment, and I wonder whether the fate of the 2008 Yirrkala Petition will be any different. Yet I also consider how far Australia has come, within my own lifetime, towards recognising Indigenous rights and taking responsibility for past injustices. And I am thankful to Yothu Yindi for opening my mind to how much further we can yet travel together.

So I hope this book succeeds in opening the minds of others to new ways of experiencing the genius of Yothu Yindi, and the traditional, historical and cross-cultural dimensions of this band's work. I hope that it helps people to listen to Yothu Yindi's music with fresh ears, to see new details in their music videos and album covers, and reflect on the words that Mandawuy has so generously shared within these pages as you follow the musical scores. And I hope that the vitality and importance of Australia's living Indigenous traditions will become apparent to all.

As I sing my final words in this book, I am again reminded of a dream that a friend of mine first sung two decades ago. It is a simple dream that anyone can sing. A dream of the synergy that grows wherever different currents meet. The dream of a brighter day when the waters will be one.

dancing trees: an epilogue

Marcia Langton

Dancing trees, sacred sunsets, whispering leaves. Spider webs in the grass glistening with dew, early morning mists hovering over the land. Such wonderful mind-pictures are just a few within the rich panoply of the Yolŋu celebration of life. For the Yolŋu, words have power, especially the esoteric words used in the lyrics of their *Manikay*, which are also used to great effect under Mandawuy Yunupiŋu's leadership in Yothu Yindi. The powerful influence of Yothu Yindi's body of work in Australia and around the world is inestimable. The band has performed all over the world and been heard by millions. But that they have brought such powerful Yolŋu words and the mind-pictures they carry to so many people, is a special achievement.

When few had heard of the Yolŋu or of Arnhem Land, Yothu Yindi's message struck a chord, as it were, with their magical combination of traditional musical forms and popular postmodern styles. It brought into the imaginations of their audiences a beautiful, complex and mysterious culture bound up with magnificent land-and-seascapes, rich in history and human thought. Its message was so different from the conventional idea of an Aboriginal people. Listeners were asked to imagine a life that was beautiful, to wonder about ideas carried in metaphors, to hear sounds with profound meanings, and to feel Mandawuy's emotional bond with his ancestors and all that they have given in this world.

Through Yothu Yindi, the Gumatj *mala* and the Rirratjiŋu *mala* have contributed a wealth of philosophy, music, art, and new ideas to the world over the past quarter-century. Alongside this band, they have come to offer another unprecedented gift, the Garma Festival of Traditional Culture, at which they present public ceremony for the Gumatj homeland of Gulkula, and teach visitors from all over the world about Yolŋu culture, religion and philosophy.

Those who have attended this festival have learnt from direct experience about the hidden values of Yolŋu culture. The elaborate meanings behind each song and dance, each intricate design painted on a body or a hollow log coffin. Most strikingly, they have seen the personal effort, commitment and investment of each dancer who pounds the sand and leaps up, kicking up fine streams of white dust, calling up the ancestors with great reverence, passion and joy. They have also learnt about the history of Arnhem Land; the missions that were established at Miliŋinbi, Yirrkala and Gali-win'ku; the anthropologists, art collectors and adventurers who visited the region; the government officials, cattle men and traders; and the long history of Yolŋu relations with the Makassan seafarers who came annually from Sulawesi in eastern Indonesia (Macknight 1976).

The northern coastline of Australia is a much contested zone of ideas, both colonial and postcolonial, about the borders of the Australia's sovereignty and security. From the time of European discovery in the 1600s, to the sea journey of Matthew Flinders in the early 1800s and the first imposition of taxes on Makassan seafarers later that century, the Aboriginal presence along Austra-lia's northern coast has been disregarded as irrelevant to the nation-building project. Yet from the northern coastal edges of the Austra-lian nation, Yothu Yindi's songs reached out to the postcolonial cities and centres where the political and social ideas of the modern Australian nation were sustained. Perhaps their words were con-veyed in an asymmetrical dialogue. But no postcolonial assumption of right could diminish the power and antiquity of the metaphors and ideas of Yothu Yindi's lyrics and its roots in *Manikay*. These were inherited from Yolŋu forebears who lived long before the British invaded.

The Garma Festival unites different Yolŋu *mala* under the Law of the ancestral figure Ganbulapula, who transformed their social world at a funeral ceremony that once took place in the ancestral past. Along with this central theme of mortuary rites that guide the souls of the deceased back home, are several themes of religious and social significance that further unite the Yolŋu *mala* as a regional polity. One of these ceremonial themes concerns their centuries-old relations with the Makassan seafarers. The Gumatj were one of the many coastal *mala* in Arnhem Land who welcomed the Makassans and found a place for them in Yolŋu society. Their harvesting and preparation of trepang was conducted throughout the monsoonal months, as the Makassan arrived in their prahus with the northwest monsoon winds and returned when the winds turned back at the end of this season. Cooked and smoked in large open vats, they were traded to China where they remain a favoured aphrodisiac and gastronomical delicacy. The history of the annual Makassan visits to Arnhem Land, dating from perhaps the seventeenth century, and the deep social connections that they made with the Yolŋu inform *mala* identities, languages and ceremonial traditions, as well as the regional sense of the polity to this day (Palmer 2000: 9–10). Evidence of the endurance of the Makassan influence abounds in Arnhem Land, and this is particularly important in the meanings of ritual emblems and trade objects.

Following the introduction of taxes levied against Makassan prahus by the South Australian government, Makassan trade with Aboriginal peoples drew to a close. In contrast to the entry of the Europeans into the region, Yolŋu today regard this period of Makassan trade as one of negotiated relationships built on equality. For the Aboriginal peoples of north Australia who encountered the Makassans long before the British arrived, they deduce from their history of this important past that they were forebears had been 'business people' who were engaged in the commerce of international trade. This inference counters the much-resented official accounts of Aboriginal life as isolated and static. This celebrated historical relationship stands in contrast to the treatment of Aboriginal people by the early frontiersmen who were still involved in armed conflict with Aborigines in Arnhem Land in the 1930s and 1940s, and to the status of Aboriginal people in the modern nation-state.

For the thousands of visitors to the Garma Festival who discover just how recent the last frontier violence against Aboriginal peoples was, and who witness the ceremonies of a religion that they were taught had long ago disappeared, a profound postcolonial dilemma is presented. It is difficult for them to ignore the fact that a dynamic Aboriginal presence continues in Australia's north, and that a customary governmentality that commemorates its own past exists.

Even more troubling is that there were people who came to Australia before the British and established long term relationships with Aboriginal people that were not colonial or oppressive. This confronts the Australian national and foundational mythology of the supposed discovery of Australia by Captain James Cook in 1770. The Makassans made no colonial declaration of sovereignty over Australia. They paid regard to local concepts of property and native title, and there was no exploitative economic relationship leading to Aboriginal impoverishment. In coastal Arnhem Land communities today, people commonly point to the positive relationships formed in the Makassan times, which spanned family ties, exchanges of words and names, and cooperative work and trade relations. Indeed, the marriage and consort relations 'negotiated' between Makassan men and Aboriginal women established 'blood ties' that are recognised by Yolŋu families to this day.

As a relationship of exchange and alliance, the Makassan–Yolŋu engagement was premised on something very different to the cultural unilateralism of the next colonial wave of visitors to Yolŋu country. Despite persistent attempts by Yolŋu to engage politically and economically with these colonists, they remain dissatisfied with the response from modern Australia. As anthropologist Ian McIntosh writes:

> The ability of Aborigines to apply their cultural repertoire as a means of fostering relations with the Makassan 'Other', also provides a powerful commentary on the nature of relations between Aborigines and non-Aborigines in Australia today. Despite a similarly disastrous contact in the early years of colonisation, the question still needs to be asked, how can the various parties come together? What laws bind the various parties as 'one'? (McIntosh 1996b: 243)

In 2005, a group of Makassans descended from those who visited hundreds of years ago, reunited with their Yolngu neighbours at the Garma Festival. The men performed music with voices, shawm and drums, while young women danced with veils. Like their ancestors who came to Australia, their culture carries influences of the Islamic faith. Ethnomusicologist Peter Toner explains how, through this connection, Dhaḻwaŋu *Manikay* also possesses melodic similarities to classical Arabic religious music, and how the particular subject *garurru* 'red flag' symbolises the 'ancestral figure called Birrinydji, the Swordman, who instituted all aspects of Dhaḻwaŋu culture normally attributed to the historical period of Makassan contact' (2001: 2–4). He also notes that the flag is a particularly important symbol here, as are the ship, the anchor and the sword. The many differently coloured flags with which specific Yolŋu *mala* still identify today stand as reminders of the many fleets of prahu that used to trade on their beaches. They remind us that at least a hundred years before Cook arrived at Botany Bay, the Yolŋu were involved in an expansive network of trade stretching from the Middle East to China via the East Indies.

I lived for many years in the Northern Territory. The honour of writing an epilogue for this important book has reminded me of an instance of the resonance of the Makassan past that is still remembered and commemorated by Yolŋu today. Watching the Darwin harbour in the mornings or the evenings, one would often see the traditional fishing vessels of Indonesian poachers, confiscated by the Australian Customs Service, burning on the water. They were set alight by the customs officers on the grounds of preventing disease and alien insect invasions, but it is clear that there was a punitive element in these peremptory actions. The livelihood of a family or small village turned to embers drifting across the sky on the breezes. The trans-generational wealth and tradition represented by these small boats cannot be estimated. Perhaps the Yolŋu histories of the Makassans give us some indication of what has been lost, as so beautifully echoed in 'Makassan Crew' by Yothu Yindi. Opening the band's final album, *Garma*, the emotional or affective register of Yolŋu religious references throughout this song's lyrics adds a piquancy to its lamentation of the past.

This history provides the context for one of Yothu Yindi's most famous songs, 'Treaty', which recounts Prime Minister Hawke's broken promise of a Treaty with Indigenous Australians. Just like 'Makassan Crew', this song laments what might have been. Galarrwuy Yunupiŋu, who was central to the 1988 Barunga State-ment's call for such a Treaty, has often reflected on this incident in his own work and music. In 'Luku-Wäŋawuy Manikay 1788' on the band's first album, *Homeland Movement*, he remains adamant that Yolŋu Law can only work if Yolŋu are recognised as the owners of their homelands, and that along with these homelands, traditional *Manikay* and *Buŋgul* 'go hand in hand as one'. Yolŋu feel, with great justification, that there remains much to be done to satisfy their demands for such recognition and respect, and until there is evidence of such, they hold the Australian nation to account for its inadequate conceptualisation of the place of their people in it.

Mandawuy, Galarrwuy, and their elder sister Gulumbu, an award-winning visual artist, grew up under the tutelage of their father, Mungurrawuy, and their mother, Makurrŋu. In his moving recent essay for *The Monthly* (Yunupiŋu 2009), Galarrwuy tells a story of disappointment and frustration from the period of their childhood, when missionaries and government officials instigated rapid change at Yirrkala, to a pivotal ceremony they held for Prime Minister Kevin Rudd to present him with the 2008 Yirrkala Peti-tion. Its avuncular tone cautions fellow Yolŋu that no government or well-intentioned outsider can 'put your life right for you' (Yunupiŋu 2009: 40). As an alternative, he states:

> I am trying to light the fire in our young men and women. We are setting fires to our own lives as we really should, and the flame will burn and intensify—an immense smoke, cloud-like and black, will arise, which will send off a signal and remind people that we, the Gumatj people, are the people of the fire.
> (Yunupiŋu 2009: 40)

Gurtha, the element of 'Fire', is intrinsically linked to Gumatj identity and to the powerful ancestral beings that reside within their homelands. Fire in the sunset is a recurring theme, along with the spark of truth that this imagery symbolises. This relationship for the Gumatj Yolŋu is preordained. It exists before Gumatj individual enters the world at birth and it remains after their death. It is this unbreakable link with the sacred past that Galarrwuy recognises as an essential characteristic of the Aboriginal citizen. We must ask what right the Australian nation-state has to override this ancestral relationship and seek to reshape human beings according to its own colonial history.

To say that the Gumatj are 'people of the fire' is to address the core of their social being as shaped by the powerful influences of the sacred history bequeathed by their ancestors (Yunupiŋu 2009: 40). Galarrwuy has brought this power to bear on the modern Yolŋu predicament in the hope of persuading Prime Minister Rudd to face the essential truth that the Australian government must enter into a just settlement with the continent's Indigenous peoples. His address to the Melbourne Law School advocated that only constitutional recognition for the rights and status of Australia's Indigenous peoples can resolve this injustice.

> When Captain Cook landed on the Australian continent he had with him an order from King George the Third. That Order was that he obtain the CONSENT of the local people to his arrival and any settlement. The Order said: 'You are also, with the Consent of the Natives, to take Possession of Convenient Situations in the Country in the Name of the King of Great Britain'. Captain Cook, and Captain Phillip after, him ignored that order. And of course it was not too long before he was in open conflict with the local Aboriginal people. The Eora people who owned Port Jackson and Sydney did not recognise the Crown's claims to ownership, just as so many Aboriginal people today still do not recognise those claims. Cook's actions were on behalf of the King, and he left a legacy that the nation is still trying to tackle

today. Indigenous peoples have their own laws and societies. For my people, it is ROM-WATANU ['Holding the
Law']. Rom-Waṯaŋu is the law of the land and the seas, and
of life itself. My people are, and will always be, the owners
and the makers of the land and sea. Rom-Waṯaŋu is the
most powerful and real thing in Yolŋu life. We do not pledge
allegiance to the Crown. Captain Phillip, and those that
followed him, failed to understand this. They failed to
establish a proper order or balance, and this has been
tearing away at the heart of the nation ever since. (Yunupiŋu
2007: 3–5)

The right to pay allegiance to the life-giving forces of the Yolŋu
world, and the right to have their own sacred beliefs, practices and
inherited ownership of homelands recognised. Until such rights
are recognised, Indigenous peoples will remain trapped in a
nineteenth century absolutist notion of the colonised citizen,
which underlies the politics of our inferior status in the Australian
nation-state. Legal recognition of our rights in this country falls far
short of developments in nations like Canada and New Zealand,
where treaties and modern agreements provide not only Indigenous rights, but also an honourable basis for the sovereignty of the
Crown. Yothu Yindi carries this fire, the truth of this important
message, within its powerful music. The story of this search for
justice is a compelling aspect of Yothu Yindi's legacy to the world,
and as this book reveals, it imbues the band's body of work with
the beauty, dignity and hope echoed here in the words of the 2008
Yirrkala Petition.

We, the united clans of east Arnhem Land, through our
most senior ḏilak 'elders', do humbly petition you, the 26th
Prime Minister of Australia, in your capacity as first
amongst equals in the Australian Parliament, and as chief
advisor to Her Majesty Queen Elizabeth the Second, to
secure within the Australian Constitution the recognition
and protection of our full and complete right to:

- our way of life in all its diversity;
- our property, being the lands and waters of east Arnhem Land;
- economic independence, through the proper use of the riches of our lands and waters in all their abundance and wealth;
- control of our lives and responsibility for our children's future.

These rights are self-evident. These rights are fundamental to our place within the Australian nation. We ask for your leadership to have the Commonwealth Parliament start the process of recognition of these rights through serious constitutional reform. (Yunupiŋu et al. 2008)

acknowledgement

I am indebted to Lisa Palmer and Odette Mazel, who have previously written about Makassan relationships with the Yolŋu, for their permission to use material from our earlier publications (Langton, Mazel & Palmer 2006). I am also indebted to the Bundanon Trust for their generous support in providing a retreat for me to write this essay.

appendices

*wa**n**a mala*

Gäpirri 'Stringray' as two Gumatj mothers with their Dhuwa children (Galarrwuy Yunupiŋu 1991).

glossary

selected terms

Balanda	European; Euro-Australian
bathi	basket; sacred baskets represent the sovereign authority given each *mala* by the original ancestors
Bayini	mysterious fair-skinned foreigners whose contact with Yolŋu predates Makassan contact by several centuries
biḻma	paired sticks used by male signers to accompany *Manikay*
Buŋgul	Dances; traditional dances belonging to each *mala* that accompany *Manikay*; full ceremonial performance
ḏämbu	head; the distinct melodic of a *Manikay* series
Dhuwa	one of the two Yolŋu constitutions founded by the original ancestors
Djaṯpaŋarri	a traditional style of improvisatory song and dance popular with youths at Yirrkala between the 1930s and the 1970s
djikuŋguṉ	yellow foam; created on Yirritja homelands at *gaṉma* sites where saltwater and freshwater currents converge
djuŋgayi	ceremonial manager; role performed by experienced leaders for their mother's *mala*
gakal	shin; refers to exposed soloist dances performed to invoke the fierce power of the original ancestors to mark important ceremonial acts
gaṉma	converging currents; sites on Yirritja homelands where saltwater and freshwater currents meet
garma	public; traditional knowledge that can be openly shared; traditional ceremonies that can be attended by all
gurruṯu	family; the primary Yolŋu kinship system
gutharra	a female's daughter's child; a male's sister's daughter's child

ḻikan	elbow; refers to the specific branch of ancestral authority held by each *mala*
ḻiya-waŋa	head-speech; the unaccompanied sung coda of an individual *Manikay* item
Maḏayin	Sacred Beauty; the hereditary body of *Yäku*, *Manikay*, *Buŋgul* and *Miny'tji* belonging to each *mala* as given by the original ancestors in distinct sets of cross-cutting subjects for each homeland
makarr	thigh; the accompanied main lyrics of an individual *Manikay* item
mala	group; specifically a group of land-owners and law-holders constituted by the original ancestors who passes ownership of its homelands and *Maḏayin* from father to child
Manikay	Songs; traditional songs performed in series of short items belonging to each *mala*
Maŋgatharra	Makassan traders who sailed annually from Sulawesi between the mid-seventeenth and early twentieth centuries
märi	a mother's mother
märipulu	a mother's mother's *mala*
matha	tongue; the dialect spoken by each *mala* as distinguished by its distinct set of *Yäku*
milkarri	crying; stylised crying songs sung by women that share the same melodic and lyrical content as men's *Manikay* items
Miny'tji	Designs; colour; traditional designs belonging to each *mala* including paintings, sculptures and fibre works
mokuy	ghost
ŋäṉdipulu	a mother's *mala*
ŋapipi	a mother's brother
ŋurru-waŋa	humming; the unaccompanied hummed introduction of an individual *Manikay* item
Rom	Law passed by the original ancestors to their human descendants

wakupulu	a female's child's *mala*; a male's sister's child's *mala*
wäŋa	country including lands and waters; the homelands belonging to each *mala*
wäŋa-ŋaraka	bone country; the main homelands belonging to each *mala*
waŋarr	the original ancestors
warwu	sorrow; an emotional aesthetic of the *Manikay* tradition
Wuymu	Pacific Islander whalers
Yäku	Names; the distinct sets of sacred names belong to each *mala*
yapapulu	sister *mala*; technically a mother's mother's mother's mother's *mala*
yiḏaki	didjeridu; played by males to accompany *Manikay*
Yirritja	one of the two Yolŋu constitutions founded by the original ancestors
Yolŋu	Person; Human; the hereditary owners of northeast Arnhem Land
Yolŋu-Matha	People's Tongues; a collective name for the different *matha* spoken by all *mala*
Yothu-yindi	child and mother
yuṯa	new; describes new *Manikay* items composed for performance in informal contexts

selected groups

Dhuwa	Ḏäṯiwuy	Yirritja	Dhalwaŋu
	Djapu'		Gumatj
	Gälpu		Maŋgalili
	Rirratjiŋu		Wangurri

selected subjects

Sacred subjects are often owned by multiple *mala* under the same constitution. The *mala* alignments cited here pertain only those directly relevant to songs discussed in this book.

Bäru	Saltwater Crocodile (Gumatj)
Baywara	Olive Python (Gälpu)
djäpana	coral sunset (Gumatj)
Djulpan	the Pleiades 'Seven Sisters' (Gumatj)
Ganbulapula	an ancestral *mokuy* hunter (Gumatj)
Gäpirri	Stingray (Gumatj)
guku	honey (Gumatj)
gurtha	fire (Gumatj)
laykarrambu	male red kangaroo (Gumatj)
mambulmambul	red kangaroo meat (Gumatj)
mända	octopus (Gumatj)
Maralitja	Saltwater Crocodile Man (Gumatj)
mätjala	driftwood (Gumatj); the Dhuwa children of Gumatj women
mulpiya'	wallaby (Rirratjiŋu)
ŋerrk	sulphur-crested cockatoo (Gumatj)
nyiŋanyiŋa	anchovy (Gumatj)
wärrarra	blood red sunset (Gumatj)
Wirrili	Yellow Ochre Man (Gumatj)
yirrmala	hull of the Bayini boat (Gumatj)

discography

* songs with music videos

(I) Homeland Movement, 1989

1   'Mainstream' *
2   'Yolŋu Woman'
3   'Homeland Movement'
4   'Djäpana: Sunset Dreaming'
5   'Gama<u>da</u>la [red kangaroo escarpment]"'
6   'Garrtjambal "Red Kangaroo"'
7   'Mambu<u>l</u>mambu<u>l</u> "Red Kangaroo Meat"'
8   'Gu<u>d</u>urrku "Brolga"' *
9   'Barrwula [a sacred waterhole]', part 1
10 'Barrwu<u>l</u>a [a sacred waterhole]', part 2'
11 'Barrwu<u>l</u>a [a sacred waterhole]', part 3'
12 'Gunmarra "Anchovy"', sequence 1
13 'Gunmarra "Anchovy"', sequence 2
14 '<u>L</u>uku-Wäŋawuy Manikay "Sovereignty Song" 1788'

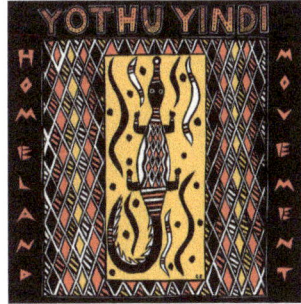

Mushroom D19520

(II) *Tribal Voice*, 1991

1   'Gapu "Water"'
2   'Treaty' *
3   'Djäpana: Sunset Dreaming'
4   'My Kind of Life'
5   'Maralitja: Crocodile Man'
6   'Dhum'thum "Agile Wallaby"'
7   'Tribal Voice' *
8   'Mainstream'
9   'Dharpa "Tree"'
10 'Yinydjapana "Dolphin"'
11 'Mätjala "Driftwood"'
12 'Hope'
13 'Gäpirri "Stingray"'

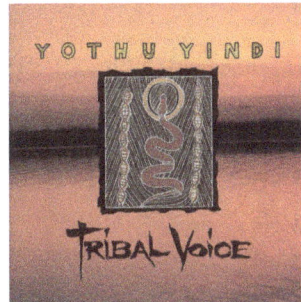

Mushroom D30602

extended edition, 1992

14 'Biyarrmak "Comic"'
15 'Treaty', Radio Mix *
16 'Djäpana: Sunset Dreaming', Radio Mix*

Mushroom TVD91017

(III) *Freedom*, 1993

1   'Timeless Land' *
2   'World of Innocence'
3   'Freedom'
4   'Baywara "Olive Python"'
5   'Ŋerrk "Sulphur-Crested Cockatoo"'
6   'Back to Culture'
7   'World Turning' *
8   'Mabo'
9   'Milika "Diamond Fish"'
10 'Daŋultji "Brolga"'
11 'Gunitjpirr Man'
12 'Yolŋu Boy'
13 'Dots on the Shells' *
14 'Our Generation'
15 'Gany'tjurr "White-Faced Heron"'
16 'Gapu "Water"', Tidal Mix *

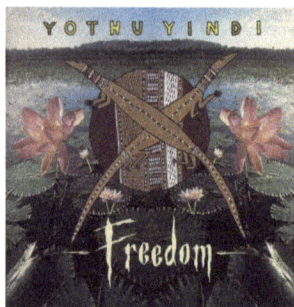

Mushroom TVD93380

(IV) *Birrkuḏa 'Honeybee': Wild Honey*, 1996

1   'Tears for Law: Garrathiya Run'
2   'Yolŋu Woman'
3   'Ŋarrpiya "Octopus"'
4   'Superhighway' *
5   'Bäpaŋ "Driftwood"'
6   'Djaṯpa'
7   'Timor'
8   'Matter of Choice'
9   'Stop That'
10 'Lorrpu "Sulphur-Crested Cockatoo"'
11 'Spirit of Peace'
12 'Yirrmala "Hull"'
13 'Honey: Birrkuḏa "Honeybee"'
14 'Cora [an old supply barge]'
15 'Mice and Men'

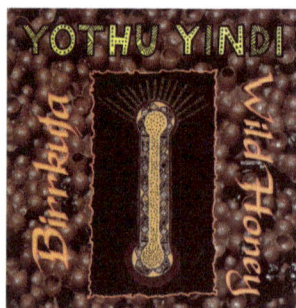

Mushroom TVD93461

(V) *One Blood*, 1999

1 'Laykarrambu "Male Red Kangaroo"'
2 'One Blood'
3 'Mainstream'
4 'World Turning'
5 'Baywara "Olive Python"'
6 'Dots on the Shells'
7 'Rräma "Coral Sunset Clouds"'
8 'Djäpana: Sunset Dreaming'
9 'Written on a Bark'
10 'Tribal Voice'
11 'Seven Sisters'
12 'Miŋamiŋa "Cycad Nut Bread"'
13 'Tears for Law: Garrathiya Run'
14 'Bäru "Saltwater Crocodile"'
15 'Belief on the Future'
16 'Nyiŋanyiŋa "Anchovy"'
17 'Our Land'
18 'Yarryurru "Red Kangaroo Spear"'
19 'Treaty '98'

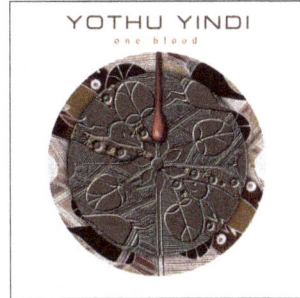

Mushroom MUSH33229 2

(VI) *Garma*, 2000

1 'Makassan Crew'
2 'Fire'
3 'Surfing the Log'
4 'Community Life' *
5 'Bush'
6 'Ghost Spirits' *
7 'Romance at Garma'
8 'Good Medicine'
9 'Calling Every Nation'
10 'Wirrkul "Maiden" Girl'
11 'Lonely Tree'
12 'Gone is the Land'
13 'Silver Owl'
14 'Guwalny "Squid": Silver Light'

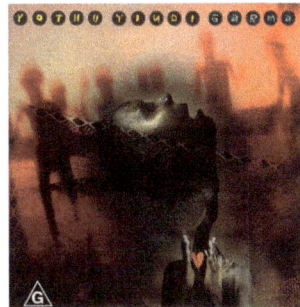

Mushroom MUSH332822

Diṯimurru 'Shimmering', 1992

This is an early compilation of music videos for songs from *Homeland Movement* and *Tribal Voice*. There would be no compilation of later videos. However, *Garma* was released as an enhanced CD with the new music-videos for 'Community Life' (VI/4) and 'Ghost Spirits' (VI/6)

1   'Treaty'
2   'Mainstream'
3   'Guḏurrku "Brolga"'
4   'Treaty', Radio Mix
5   'Djäpana: Sunset Dreaming', Radio Mix
6   'Tribal Voice'

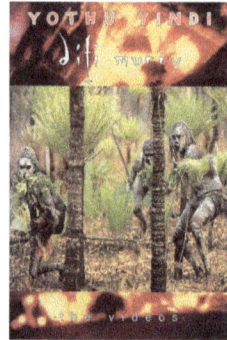

Mushroom V81305

Yolŋu Boy, 2000

Directed by Stephen Johnson of Burrundi Pictures, this motion picture was produced in collaboration with the Yothu Yindi Foundation and the Australian Children's Television Foundation. Galarrwuy and Mandawuy worked as Associate Producers, and contributed to its original soundtrack. 'Yolŋu Boy' (III/12) was Mandawuy's second original song.

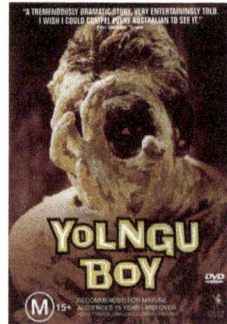

Palace Films
22054SDW

Contemporary Masters Series, 2001–03

This collection of albums features traditional repertoires performed some of Arnhem Land's most renowned ceremonial musicians.

(i) *Gobulu 'Grave'* (2001) is a Gumatj *Manikay* performed by Galarrwuy Yunupiŋu (voice, *biḻma*) and Malŋay Yunupiŋu (*yiḏaki*).

(ii) *Waḻuka 'Rain'* (2001) is a Gälpu *Manikay* series performed by Gurritjiri Gurruwiwi (voice, *biḻma*) and Djalu Gurruwiwi (*yiḏaki*).

(iii) *Djalu Teaches and Plays Yiḏaki* vol. 1 (2001). On this CD, Djalu Gurruwiwi, Ḻarrtjaŋa Gurruwiwi

Yothu Yindi
Foundation YYF 1–6

and Barrnyulnyul Yunupiŋu teach *yidaki* accompaniments to Gälpu and Dhalwaŋu *Manikay* series.

(iv) *Mamba 'Sand Crab'* (2001) is a Rirratjiŋu *Manikay* series performed by Ralkurru Marika (voice, *bilma*), Malŋay Yunupiŋu (*yidaki*) and Narripapa Yunupiŋu (*yidaki*).

(v) *Nundhirribala* (2001). The Nunggubuyu are an Indigenous people of southeast Arnhem Land. They speak Wubuyu and the Nundhirribala are one of their land-owning groups. This CD features a Nundhirribala song series performed by Mungayana Nundhirribala (voice, *wilbilg* 'paired sticks') and Yadu Numamudidi (*lhambilbilg* 'didjeridu').

(vi) *Djalu Teaches and Plays Yidaki* vol. 2 (2003). On this CD, Djalu Gurruwiwi and Larrtjaŋa Gurruwiwi teach *yidaki* accompaniments to two Gälpu *manikay* series.

chronology

∞	The original ancestors name, shape and populate the Yolŋu homelands.
c11,000 BP	The sea level rises and rapidly engulfs Yolŋu homelands.
c1400	The Bayini visit Arnhem Land.
1602–1939	The Balanda 'Dutch' occupy the East Indies 'Indonesia'.
1623	Two Balanda 'Dutch' vessels commanded by Jan Cartensz, the Pera and the Arnhem, navigate Arnhem Land.
c1700	Heightened relations between the Yolŋu and Makassan traders from Sulawesi commence.
1864	250,000 acres of the Northern Territory, including the whole of Arnhem Land, is auctioned sight unseen by the Colony of South Australia to investors in Adelaide and London.
1872–c1940	Pastoral wars devastate peoples of Arnhem Land.
1901	The federation of the Colonies into the Commonwealth of Australia.
1906	Makassan trade ends when the state government of South Australia, then responsible for the Northen Territory, imposes steep tariffs on foreign vessels entering its waters.
1911–78	Administration of the Northern Territory passes from South Australia to the Commonwealth.
1923	The first Christian mission to the Yolŋu is established by the Methodists at Miliŋinbi.
1931	Following two decades of hesitation, the Commonwealth declares Arnhem Land an Aboriginal Reserve.
1933–34	Dhäkiyarr Wirrpanda is extradited to Darwin, tried and sentenced to death for the alleged murder of Constable Albert McColl. He is released on appeal but mysteriously disappears that same night, never to be found.
1934	The second Methodist mission to the Yolŋu is established at Yirrkala.
1942	The third Methodist mission to the Yolŋu is established at Galiwin'ku.

c1955	Yolŋu families begin to use short-wave radios to intercept Radio Australia and stations in Darwin.
1962	Sixteen leaders from nine Yolŋu groups of the Gove Peninsula create the Yirrkala Church Panels, which come to symbolise their solidarity against the proposed NABALCO bauxite mine.
1963	Yolŋu leaders send the Yirrkala Petition to the House of Representatives in protest against the proposed NABALCO bauxite mine.
1968	The NABALCO bauxite mine goes into production.
	Yolŋu leaders send the Wuyal Petition to the House of Representatives to protest the proposed renaming of Nhulunbuy.
1968–71	Yolŋu leaders from Yirrkala take their dispute against the NABALCO bauxite mine with the Supreme Court of the Northern Territory, but are ultimately defeated.
1970	Soft Sands forms at Galiwin'ku.
1970–96	*The Yirrkala Film Project* directed by Ian Dunlop documents the impact of mining on the Yolŋu community at Yirrkala.
1971	Galarrwuy Yunupiŋu releases a single of 'Gurindji Blues' by Ted Egan with a spoken introduction by the Aboriginal rights activist Vincent Lingiari.
1972–74	The Aboriginal Land Rights Commission investigates the loss of the Yolŋu case against the NABALCO bauxite mine, though government ignores most of its recommendations.
1973	The Northern Land Council is established.
	The final Methodist mission to the Yolŋu is established at Ramanginiŋ.
	Prime Minister Gough Whitlam implements a new policy of self-management for Indigenous communities.
1974	Mandawuy experiences his first rock concert at the Sydney Opera House.
1976	The Commonwealth passes the *Aboriginal Land Rights (Northern Territory) Act*. Under this act, Arnhem Land becomes an Aboriginal Land Trust and the Northern Land Council is charged with its enforcement.

1977	The Methodist Church of Australasia joins the Uniting Church of Australia.
1977–80	Galarrwuy Yunupiŋu serves his first term as Chair of the Northern Land Council.
1978	The Northern Territory becomes self-governing.
	Galarrwuy Yunupiŋu is named Australian of the Year for his negotiations on the Ranger uranium mine agreement.
1982	Soft Sands tours North America.
1983	Mandawuy Yunupiŋu composes 'Djäpana: Sunset Dreaming' while working as Assistant Principal at Shepherdson College.
1983–2004	Galarrwuy Yunupiŋu serves subsequent terms as Chair of the Northern Land Council.
1985	Galarrwuy Yunupiŋu is made a Member of the Order of Australia.
1986	Mandawuy Yunupiŋu composes 'Mainstream' for an assignment towards his Bachelor of Arts in Education.
	Mandawuy Yunupiŋu, Stu Kellaway, Wiṯiyana Marika, Cal Williams, Milkayŋu Munuŋgurr, and Andy Beletty form Yothu Yindi in Darwin.
1987	Mandawuy Yunupiŋu is appointed Assistant Principal at the Yirrkala Community Education Centre.
	Yothu Yindi tours New South Wales.
1988	Mandawuy Yunupiŋu graduates with a Bachelor of Arts in Education from Deakin University.
	Galarrwuy Yunupiŋu and Wenten Rubuntja present the Barunga Statement to Prime Minister Hawke at the Barunga Festival.
	Yothu Yindi performs at the Seoul Cultural Olympics in Korea, and tours North America with Midnight Oil and John Trudell.
1989	Yothu Yindi releases *Homeland Movement*.
	Yothu Yindi performs in Hong Kong and Papua New Guinea, and tours Australia with Neil Young.
1990	Mandawuy Yunupiŋu is appointed Principal at the Yirrkala Community Education Centre.

1990   Yothu Yindi tours New Zealand with Tracy Chapman, and performs at the Edinburgh Fringe Festival and the European Folk Festival in Glasgow.

The Yothu Yindi Foundation is established to promote Yolŋu traditional maintenance and economic development.

Gurrumul Yunupiŋu and Jodie Cockatoo join Yothu Yindi.

1991   The Commonwealth establishes the Council for Aboriginal Reconciliation.

Yothu Yindi releases *Tribal Voice*, which wins awards from the Australian Record Industry Association (ARIA) for Australian Record of the Year and Best Indigenous Record.

'Treaty' becomes the first song in any traditional Australian language to chart anywhere, and wins awards for Song of the Year (Australasian Performing Right Association), Song Writing (Human Rights and Equal Opportunity Commission), Best Australian Single (ARIA), Best Australian Video (Australian Music Awards); and Best Australian Video (MTV International Awards).

Yothu Yindi performs at the New Music Seminar in New York and signs an international recording contract with Hollywood Records.

1992   'Treaty' is remixed by Filthy Lucre in Melbourne and *Tribal Voice* dominates Australian charts.

Yothu Yindi tours Australia, North America and Europe, and represents Australia in New York at the launch of the United Nations International Year for the World's Indigenous People.

Yothu Yindi's early videos are released on *Diṯimurru*.

Prime Minister Paul Keating delivers his moving Redfern Park Speech to launch Australia's calendar of events for the International Year for the World's Indigenous People.

Mandawuy Yunupiŋu is named Australian of the Year for his services to music and work as cultural ambassador.

Terra nullius is overturned with the Mabo judgment from the High Court of Australia.

1993   'Djäpana: Sunset Dreaming' becomes Yothu Yindi's second hit song, and wins awards from ARIA for Best Indigenous Record, Best Video and Best Engineer.

1993   Yothu Yindi joins Slim Dusty on the Raypirri Tour to promote the National Drug Offensive in Indigenous communities, and tours Australia, Japan and Europe.

The Commonwealth passes the *Native Title Act*.

1993   Yothu Yindi releases *Freedom*.

1994   'Treaty' continues to chart internationally as Yothu Yindi tours Australia, PNG, New Zealand, Germany, France, Belgium, Netherlands, Switzerland, Luxemburg, Britain, USA, Canada and Japan.

The Papuan musicians Ben Hakalitz and Buruka Tau-Matagu join Yothu Yindi.

1995   Yothu Yindi records in Australia and Britain, and tours Germany, Australia and North America.

1996   Yothu Yindi releases *Birrkuḏa: Wild Honey*.

1997   Yothu Yindi performs in South Africa and Zimbabwe for the Fred Hollows Foundation, and tours Europe and Brazil.

1998   Mandawuy Yunupiŋu is honoured as a Doctor of the University by the Queensland University of Technology for his services to Indigenous education and Aboriginal Reconciliation.

Yothu Yindi records in Dublin and Bavaria, and tours Germany with Peter Maffay on the Encounters Tour.

The Yothu Yindi Foundation hosts a preliminary workshop at Guḻkuḻa to prepare the Garma Festival of Traditional Culture.

1999   Yothu Yindi tours Vietnam, Germany, Austria, Holland, New Zealand and Australia, performs with the Darwin Symphony Orchestra, and appears at the Glastonbury Festival in Britain.

The Yothu Yindi Foundation establishes the annual Garma Festival of Traditional Culture at Guḻkuḻa, and opens the Yirrŋa Music Development Centre at Gunyaŋara.

2000   The motion picture *Yolŋu Boy* is released in association with the Yothu Yindi Foundation.

Yothu Yindi tours Australia and New Zealand with the Big Day Out, and celebrates East Timor's freedom with a concert in Dili on the first anniversary of the nation's vote for independence from Indonesia.

2000	Yothu Yindi releases *Garma*, and performs in Sydney for the Closing Ceremony of the Olympic Games and the Opening Ceremony of the Paralympic Games.
	Ownership of the NABALCO bauxite mine passes to ALCAN.
2001	Yothu Yindi performs in Melbourne at the Moomba Festival and with the Australian Youth Orchestra for the Finale of the Centenary of Federation Festival.
	The Council for Aboriginal Reconciliation becomes Reconciliation Australia.
2001–03	The Yothu Yindi Foundation releases the six-album Contemporary Masters Series.
2002	Yothu Yindi performs at Riddu Riḍḍu Festival of Sami culture in Norway.
	NABALCO ceases management of the ALCAN bauxite mine.
	The annual Symposium on Indigenous Music and Dance is established at the Garma Festival.
2003	The family of Dhäkiyarr Wirrpanda lead a traditional ceremony into the Supreme Court of the Northern Territory to lay his soul to rest, and to reconcile with the family of Constable Albert McColl.
2004	Mandawuy Yunupiŋu and Jack Thompson launch the National Recording Project for Indigenous Performance in Australia at the Garma Festival.
	Mandawuy Yunupiŋu attends the Deadlys in Sydney where he receives the Jimmy Little Award for Lifetime Achievement in Aboriginal and Torres Strait Music.
	The Garma Festival wins the Skål International Ecotourism Award for Educational Programs.
2008	Mandawuy Yunupiŋu's chronic kidney disease worsens, and Yothu Yindi gives its final concert in Darwin.

references

Attwood, Bain & Andrew Markus (eds) 1999. *The struggle for Aboriginal rights: a documentary history* (Sydney, Allen).

Bowler, Jim 1994. 'Climatic change,' in David R Horton (ed.), *The encyclopaedia of Aboriginal Australia* (Canberra, Aboriginal Studies Press).

Buku-Larrŋgay Mulka Centre 1999. *Saltwater: Yirrkala bark paintings of sea country* (Sydney, Isaacs).

Charles Darwin University 2006. 'Charles Darwin University Yolŋu Studies' <http://learnline.cdu.edu.au/yolngustudies> viewed 4 February 2009.

Collins, Allan & Tom Murray (dirs) 2004. *Dhäkiyarr versus the king* (Film Australia)

Cooke, Michael. 1996. 'The Makassan influence,' in Michael Cooke (ed.), *Aboriginal languages in contemporary contexts: Yolŋu-Matha at Galiwin'ku* (Batchelor, Batchelor College) pp. 1–20.

Corn, Aaron 2007. 'To see their fathers' eyes: expressions of ancestry through *yarraṯa* among Yolŋu popular bands from Arnhem Land, Australia,' in Freya Jarman-Ivens (ed.), *Oh Boy! Masculinities and popular music* (Oxford, Routledge) pp. 77–99.

Corn, Aaron (ed.) 2007. 'The National Recording Project for Indigenous Performance in Australia' <http://www.aboriginalartists.com.au/NRP.htm> viewed 4 February 2009.

Corn, Aaron with Neparrŋa Gumbula 2005. 'Ancestral precedent as creative inspiration: the influence of Soft Sands on popular song composition in Arnhem Land', in Graeme Ward & Adrian Muckle (eds), *The power of knowledge, the resonance of tradition: electronic publication of papers from the AIATSIS conference, September 2001* (Canberra, AIATSIS) pp. 31–68.

Corn, Aaron & Neparrŋa Gumbula 2004. 'Now Balanda say we lost our land in 1788: challenges to the recognition of Yolŋu Law in contemporary Australia', in Marcia Langton et al. (eds), *Honour among Nations? Treaties and agreements with Indigenous peoples* (Melbourne, Melbourne University Publishing) pp. 101–16.

—— 2006. '*Rom* and the Academy repositioned: binary models in Yolŋu intellectual traditions and their application to wider intercultural dialogues,' in Lynette Russell (ed.), *Boundary writing: an exploration of race, culture and gender binaries in contemporary Australia* (Honolulu, University of Hawai'i Press) pp. 170–97.

—— 2007. '*Buḏutthun ratja wiyinymirri*: formal flexibility in the Yolŋu Manikay tradition and the challenge of recording a complete repertoire,' *Australian Aboriginal Studies* 2007(2): 116–27.

Dunlop, Ian (dir.) 1970–96. *The Yirrkala film project* (Film Australia).

Knopoff, Steven 1992. '*Yuḏa Manikay*: juxtaposition of ancestral and contemporary elements in the performance of Yolŋu clan songs,' *Yearbook for Traditional Music* 24: 138–53.

Langton, Marcia, Odette Mazel & Lisa Palmer 2006. 'The "spirit" of the thing: the boundaries of Aboriginal economic relations at Australian common law,' *Australian Journal of Anthropology* 17: 307–21.

Macknight, CC 1976. *The Voyage to Marege': Makassan trepangers in Northern Australia* (Melbourne, Melbourne University Publishing).

Magowan, Fiona 2007. *Melodies of mourning: music and emotion in Northern Australia* (Santa Fe, SAR Press).

Marika, Wandjuk 1995. *Wandjuk Marika: life story as told to Jennifer Isaacs* (Brisbane, University of Queensland Press).

McIntosh, Ian S 1996a. 'Islam and Australia's Aborigines? A perspective from northeast Arnhem Land,' *Journal of Religious History* 20: 53–77.

—— 1996b. '"Can we be equal in your eyes?": a perspective on reconciliation from north-east Arnhem Land', PhD thesis, Northern Territory University.

Mountford, Charles P 1956. *Records of the American-Australian scientific expedition to Arnhem Land* (Melbourne, Melbourne University Publishing) vol 1.

Mundine, Djon 1998. 'The native born,' in *The native born: objects and representations from Ramanginiŋ, Arnhem Land* (Sydney, Museum of Contemporary Art) pp. 29–111.

Palmer, Lisa 2000. '*Trepang* opening night: dramatising shared histories,' *Arena* 45: 9–10.

Read, Peter 2005. 'Dhäkiyarr Wirrpanda: appeal for justice,' *Uncommon lives from the National Archives of Australia* <http://uncommonlives. naa.gov.au/life.asp?lID=2> viewed 4 February 2009.

Sharp, Nonie 1996. *No ordinary judgment* (Canberra, Aboriginal Studies Press).

Skinnyfish Music 2009. 'The masters series' <http://www.skinnyfishmusic. com.au/index.php?option=com_content&task=view&id=15&Itemid= 35> viewed 4 February 2009.

Supreme Court of the Northern Territory 1971. 'Milirrpum and others versus NABALCO Pty Ltd and the Commonwealth of Australia', *Federal Law Reports* 17: 141–294.

Toner, Peter G 2000. 'Ideology, influence and innovation: the impact of Makassan contact on Yolŋu music,' *Perfect Beat* 5(1): 22–41.

—— 2001. 'When the echoes are gone: a Yolŋu musical anthropology,' PhD thesis, Australian National University.

Williams, Nancy 1986. *The Yolŋu and their land: a system of land tenure and the fight for its recognition* (Canberra, AIAS).

Yothu Yindi Foundation 2006. *Garma Festival* <http://www.garma.telstra. com> viewed 4 February 2009.

Yunupiŋu, Mandawuy 1994. 'Yothu Yindi: finding balance,' *Race and Class* 35(4): 114–20.

Yunupiŋu, Mandawuy, Marcia Langton & Allan Marett (eds) 2002. 'Statement on Indigenous music and performance,' <http://www.garma. telstra.com/2002/statement-music02.htm> viewed 4 February 2009.

Yunupiŋu, Galarrwuy 2009/2008. 'Tradition, truth and tomorrow,' *The Monthly* issue 41: 32–40.

Yunupiŋu, Galarrwuy 2007. 'Serious business.' <www.bowden-mccormack. com.au/uploads/news/galarrwuy-yunupingu.pdf> viewed 4 February 2009.

Yunupiŋu, Yumbulul & Djiniyini Dhamarrandji 1997. 'My island home: a marine protection strategy for Manbuyŋa ga Rulyapa (Arafura Sea),' in Galarrwuy Yunupiŋu (ed.), *Our land is our life: land rights past, present and future* (Brisbane, University of Queensland Press) pp. 181–87.

Zorc, R David 1996. *Yolŋu-Matha dictionary*, reprint (Bachelor, Bachelor College).

about the authors

AARON CORN is a Research Fellow in Ethnomusicology and Australian Indigenous Studies at the University of Sydney. He holds a PhD in Music from the University of Melbourne and worked there in the Australian Indigenous Studies Program under the direction of Marcia Langton. Since 1996 he has collaborated with Indigenous communities in Arnhem Land on research into the application of their traditions to new cross-cultural contexts. In 2004, he established the National Recording Project for Indigenous Performance in Australia alongside Mandawuy Yunupiŋu, Allan Marett and Marcia Langton. He records Indigenous oral histories for the National Library of Australia, and teaches on Yolŋu culture at NAISDA Dance College.

MARCIA LANGTON AM is the founding Chair of Australian Indigenous Studies at the University of Melbourne. She is a prominent advocate for Indigenous rights and the co-editor of *First Australians* with Rachel Perkins (Melbourne University Publishing, 2008).

ALLAN MARETT is Professor of Ethnomusicology at the University of Sydney. He directs the National Recording Project for Indigenous Performance in Australia, and authored a seminal book on the *Wangga* song tradition of north Australia (Wesleyan University Press, 2005).

MELINDA SAWERS is the Director of Performing Arts at Wenona in North Sydney. She is a respected music educator and conductor, and the co-author of a secondary school text on Musicianship and Analysis with Deborah Smith (Smith, 2002).

GALARRWUY YUNUPIŊU AM is a highly regarded Yolŋu leader, who has worked to secure land rights and socioeconomic futures for Indigenous Australians since the early 1960s. He was Australian of the Year for 1978, chairs the Yothu Yindi Foundation, and has been recognised by the National Trust of Australia as an Australian Living National Treasure.

MANDAWUY YUNUPIŊU is the renowned founder of Yothu Yindi and the Yothu Yindi Foundation. He was the 1992 Australian of the Year and holds an honorary doctorate in Education from the Queensland University of Technology.

THE INDIGENOUS MUSIC OF AUSTRALIA

A series books and albums from Sydney University Press, presented as an initiative of

The National Recording Project
for Indigenous Performance in Australia
www.aboriginalartists.com.au/NRP.htm

BOOK SERIES edited by Allan Marett

1   *Reflections & voices: exploring the music of Yothu Yindi with Mandawuy Yunupiŋu* by Aaron Corn, 2009

2   *Wangga songs of north-west Australia: recordings, song-texts and translations in their historical and ethnographic contexts* by Allan Marett, Linda Barwick & Lys Ford, forthcoming

ALBUM SERIES edited by Linda Barwick

1   *Wurrurrumi Kun-Borrk: songs from Western Arnhem Land* by Kevin Djimarr, 2007

2   *Yindi-Yindi: Wangga songs from Belyuen* by Tommy Barrtjap, forthcoming

3   *Wangga Songs from Belyuen* by Jimmy Muluk, forthcoming

4   *Wangga Songs from Belyuen* by Bobby Lambudju Lane, forthcoming

5   *Walakandha Wangga: a Marri Tjavin song series from Wadeye* by Thomas Kungiung et al., forthcoming

6   *Ma-yawa wangga: a Marri Ammu song series from Wadeye* by Charlie Niwili Brinken & Maurice Ngulkur, forthcoming

Future volumes will cover the *Djanba* and *Lirrga* song traditions of Wadeye, the Yolŋu *Manikay* tradition, and Bongolinj-bongolinj, a series of *Kunborrk* songs from Beswick.